MW01093590

THE FOUR CORNERS ANASAZI
A Guide to Archeological Sites

by ROSE HOUK
Foreword by Stewart L. Udall

Photography & Illustrations by JIM FUGE

*San Juan National Forest Association • P.O. Box 2261
Durango, Colorado 81302 • 303-385-1210
In cooperation with the San Juan National Forest*

Design and Production by Pika Graphics • Durango, Colorado

CONTENTS

FOREWORD
by Stewart L. Udall

For most of the past 1,000 years, the remote areas where four of our states touch has been the home to a rich native culture. When passing through the Four Corners today, the casual visitor may not even be aware of the hundreds of ruins amid one of America's most severe high desert landscapes. To the untrained eye, the region may appear virtually uninhabitable.

Yet at the peak around A.D. 1250, the Four Corners was probably home to more than 50,000 Anasazi. Just fifty years later, they were gone...as far as we know every last one. This mass abandonment of an area where a great culture developed is one of the enduring mysteries of American archaeology.

The people did not disappear. Their descendants still live today in the pueblos of New Mexico and Arizona. The rich culture survives in the modern world, still recognizable in its ancient roots. Still evolving as a great living entity.

These people left no written history. Their past is recorded in the abandoned towns and villages of the Four Corners. From these meager remains, archeologists are piecing together a thousand years of Anasazi development and failure. Only a handful of the hundreds of significant sites have been scientifically excavated, but this research is beginning to reveal the extent and scope of this ancient American culture.

This handy guide takes the modern visitor to the heart of the Four Corners and its rich history of Anasazi sites. Some like Canyon de Chelly and Chimney Rock are spectacular in their settings. Others are less dramatic to the eye, but no less so in their significance. The great centers at Chaco Canyon and the Montezuma Valley show evidence of extraordinary complexity and organization. Others are the more simple homes of farming people.

I urge the new visitor to the area to take the time to see both the dramatic and the more simple. For all have much to tell us of the culture that developed here. The setting too is spectacular and very much a part of the Anasazi world. It is a world of soaring mountain peaks and dramatic valleys...of lush forest and stark deserts. It is a place that is still remote and wild—a place to be explored and treasured. It is a delicate place, so help protect it from vandals and looters. Take your time and enjoy the past!

Betatakin, Navajo National Monument

The amazing Trails of Tsankawi, Bandelier, New Mexico

PREFACE

Four Corners. The place where the states of Arizona, Utah, New Mexico, and Colorado meet in neat right angles. This unique point in the United States, put on maps by nineteenth-century cartographers, owes its existence to long-forgotten political decisions. Now the Four Corners Monument is a destination for many visitors to the Southwest, who, after long hours of desert driving, find a slightly crumbling concrete slab in the middle of nowhere.

But the Four Corners is much more than a physical marker or a spot on a map. Radiating from this point is a region filled with classic textbook geology, compelling geography, and diverse cultures. The definition and boundaries of the Four Corners region vary depending upon whom you ask. Some refer to geography or topography; others, the rocks. Still others point to the mix of people—Anglo, Hispanic, Native American—who live there.

In general, the Four Corners region is an ellipse, bounded on the east by the San Juan Mountains of southwest Colorado and the Continental Divide weaving down into New Mexico. The southern edge can be marked by an artificial boundary, Interstate 40, whose route approximately traces the natural drainages of the Puerco and Little Colorado rivers. The Colorado River angling across southeast Utah delineates the region on the west and north.

More than anything else, the Four Corners is land. Stark, beautiful, difficult, lonely and empty, given over to rock, sand, wind, clouds, and sunlight. It is colorful land, sometimes done up in garish reds, other times in the softest lavenders. It is land for stretching your eyes to a nearly endless horizon, broken perhaps eighty miles distant by the stairstep edges of mesas, the jagged tips of tilted ridges, or the round backs of high, blue mountains. Between you and the horizon lie smaller mesas, wide valleys, and unseen canyons. All of this land is embraced within the physiographic province known as the Colorado Plateau, 130,000 square miles of the world's finest exposures of sandstones, shales, and limestones, bared for all to see.

Sandstone cliffs, Southeast Utah

Little water falls on this rocky, high desert. Rainfall averages only ten inches a year, except in the highest mountains which enjoy heavy snows in winter. Ironically, this dearth of water makes the Four Corners a fantastic place for archeology. The aridity has preserved homes, baskets, pottery, tools, food and bones.

The prehistoric culture most commonly associated with the Four Corners region is the Anasazi. From around 200 B.C. until A.D. 1300, these people built their houses, grew crops, and raised families in the region. We know this much from the work of archeologists, whose job is to make history of prehistory—to establish events, places, dates, and the unique traits of a culture.

Beyond this, archeologists try to elucidate the relationships between these people and their neighbors and to determine how they changed through time—to get at the essential question of who the people really were. How the Anasazi lived in and adapted to this land and why they finally left it are the more complex questions that occupy Southwestern archeologists' minds today.

After spending any amount of time in the Four Corners country, nonscientists are likely to ask some basic questions too: What did the Anasazi find to eat in this sparse land? How did they get around in such tortuous terrain? And why did they choose this region over more forgiving places? Given their seemingly harsh environment, we might conjure an image of a primitive people, pounding on rocks and grunting at one another. But then we arrive at Cliff Palace in Mesa Verde or gaze at the exquisite masonry wall of Pueblo Bonito in Chaco Canyon and our perception

Pueblo Bonito, Chaco Canyon

changes; we begin to ask other questions about what was obviously a more elaborate, complex society than we first imagined.

And once we have seen these places and started to ask these questions, we must beware. For we may fall prey to an addiction—an incurable urge to see other sites, to gain more knowledge of the subtleties of the Anasazi, and finally to view this incredible land through their eyes. We start to ask, as we look at each rock formation, whether it would provide a good homesite or good building material. Would the mud in this streambed make fine clay for a potter's hands? Where might there be potholes that would hold water for a few days after a rain? Which soil would yield the greatest harvest of corn? How might we get those necessities, and luxuries, that we could not provide for ourselves?

Kokopellis of Shay Canyon

The pottery, fields, and harmonious pueblos of the Anasazi are well preserved in the Four Corners today. Along with these one can find thousand-year-old fingerprints in mortar, a child's toy, an animated flute player drawn on a polished boulder—all reminders of a people who built a long-lasting culture in this stark, beautiful region. So strong is their presence that if you sit quietly in the shade of a pueblo room, you may hear the voices of the Anasazi.

One of the amazing qualities of the Four Corners is the evidence there among the present day Hopi, Zuni, and Rio Grande Pueblos of an unbroken continuum from prehistoric times to the present day. What we see in the Pueblos today is not so different from what the Spaniards saw when they encountered these descendants of the Anasazi, in their pueblo homes in the sixteenth century. As art historian J. J. Brody put it, at that time in the Pueblos, "Religion permeated all things. Villages might be cosmic maps; colors, numbers, and animals were sacred, beauty itself was a prayer."

The Spaniards, drawn by the promise of gold and lost souls, were unappreciative of Pueblo culture and did their best to destroy it. But the Pueblos remained strong, their oral traditions handed down from grandparents to grandchildren, a more powerful force than any lust for material wealth. As archeologist Jim Judge has said, "Anyone who has visited any of the Pueblo communities knows that the Anasazi are alive and well in their current locations, and . . they may be doing much better than the rest of us."

In the Four Corners we can also see other Native Americans who moved in after the Anasazi had vacated their homeland. The Navajo Nation occupies a reservation of nearly seventeen million acres in northeast Arizona, northwest New Mexico, and a piece of southeast Utah. Two groups of Ute Indians—the Southern and Ute Mountain Utes—live on small reservations in southwest Colorado. These people have their own stories to tell, their own history and prehistory.

Restored roofs and courtyard of Spruce Tree House, Mesa Verde

ANASAZI CHRONOLOGY

(Pecos Classification)

1500	Pueblo IV
1400	
1300	
1200	Pueblo III
1100	
1000	Pueblo II
900	
800	Pueblo I
700	
600	Basket Maker III
500	
400	
300	
200	A.D.
100	
0	
100	Basket Maker II
200	B.C.
300	
400	
500	
600	
700	
800	Basket Maker I

THE FOUR CORNERS
ANASAZI

*B*lack clouds rolled over Cedar Mesa, and thunder shook the ground. Snakewhips of lightning lashed from the clouds, and big raindrops pelted the red earth. By sunset the storm had exhausted its energy. Low rays of sunlight diffused a silvery glow over the wet slickrock.

A young Anasazi man had taken shelter under a large alcove to wait out the storm. When it stopped, he emerged to breathe deeply of the sweet, clean air and found every pothole filled with water. Kneeling beside one of the rock basins, he scooped up a handful of water and took a drink. Never was there a more welcome gift. This water meant life—for him and his family, for his corn, and for the deer he hunted.

He had waited several weeks for such a storm. This was the time of year when the rains normally arrived, but this year they had been slow to come. His father had told him that was the way it was in this land—first calling the rain, then waiting for it to come. But the young man had not yet lived long enough to share his father's perspective, his patience with probabilities. He wanted certainty, for if the rains did not come, it would mean a long, cold, hungry winter; and he knew it would soon be upon them.

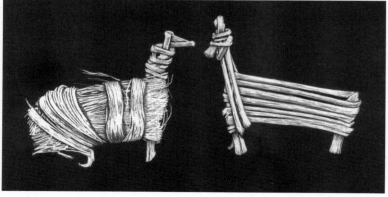

Prehistoric twig figures

Horse Collar type entrance, Grand Gulch Primitive Area

Back country ruins, Canyonlands National Park

Southern side of Taos Pueblo, Rio Pueblo de Taos in foreground

Back country site with original roofing, southeastern Utah

Cahone Group, Hovenweep National Monument—the builders carefully fitted a tower over several large boulders, the remains of which can be seen in the middle ground

North cliff of Chaco Wash, Pueblo Bonito in the distance

Corrugated and Greyware Pueblo III pottery displayed at Keet Seel, Navajo National Monument

Tower Ruins, Canyonlands National Park

People had not always worried so much about whether rains would come to water their corn. The predecessors of the Anasazi were much more mobile people, tied more directly to what nature and the seasons offered—hunting jackrabbits and mule deer and gathering piñon nuts and ricegrass. These hunter-gatherers belonged to what is known as the Desert Archaic culture. Archeologists are still looking for conclusive evidence to determine whether they were the actual ancestors of the Anasazi, or whether the Anasazi entered the Four Corners from somewhere else.

Whatever their origins, the Anasazi began to emerge as an identifiable culture around 200 B.C., and lived in the Four Corners region for at least fifteen hundred years. The Anasazi are distinguished from the earlier Desert Archaic people in two significant ways: by their more permanent dwellings and by their practice of planting crops. For the first 500 years or so the Anasazi did continue to hunt game and gather plants; but with time, agriculture began to emerge as the cornerstone of their economy.

The Anasazi became resourceful farmers and active traders. They were also expert weavers and potters, crafting beautiful baskets and manufacturing the black and white ceramics that are their signature. Their ceremonial life must have been rich indeed; they built special places to accommodate both their social and their most sacred gatherings. They carried their infants on cradleboards, causing a distinctive flattening of the back of the skull. And they

buried their dead in a distinct way as well—in shallow graves, the bodies flexed, with pottery and other grave goods accompanying them. Although they eventually settled into permanent homes and villages, the Anasazi never stopped responding to their environment—especially to the availability of water.

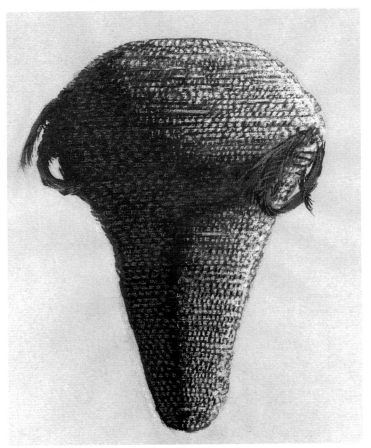

Water carrying basket
Interior lined with piñon gum, carrying loops made of human hair

THE BASKETMAKERS

Colorado rancher Richard Wetherill is best known for his discovery of Cliff Palace and Spruce Tree House in Mesa Verde on a wintry day in 1888. But that is not, by any means, the extent of his influence on Southwestern archeology. Taking time off from ranch work in the winters of 1894 and 1897, Wetherill led the Hyde Exploring Expedition into Grand Gulch, a major tributary of the San Juan River in southeast Utah.

Woven yucca sandal

In the many alcoves of this fantastic world of rock and sand, he found prehistoric remains that looked different from those of the "Cliff Dwellers" that he had seen in Mesa Verde: lovely woven baskets, sandals, mats, and nets. He called the makers of these woven goods the "Basket People." His patron, Talbot Hyde, changed this to "Basketmaker," the name that has persisted to this day. Grand Gulch remains an important example of this earliest stage of Anasazi development in the Four Corners.

Wetherill was also among the first to use the term Anasazi, the word he had heard Navajos use in describing the remains of the prehistoric people. The word has commonly been translated as "the ancient ones," though a more literal translation is "enemy ancestors." Hopi Indians have their own word for the ancient ones, *hisatsinom*. The Utes call them *mookigue*, their word for monkey, because of the way the Anasazi adeptly climbed around in their rocky home.

The name "Anasazi" entered the lexicon of archeology when Harvard University's Alfred Vincent Kidder brought it into common use. Kidder was a pioneer of Southwest archeology, arriving in the region in the early 1900s and excavating Pecos Pueblo in northern New Mexico. Legend has it that a nail in a laboratory floor at Harvard's Peabody Museum marks the spot where he and colleague Samuel J. Guernsey shook hands and said, "Let's do the Southwest." They made good on their vow, and from their work came the chronology of Anasazi development, called the Pecos Classification, which is still generally in use today.

According to this chronology, the Basketmaker period is actually a transition from Desert Archaic to Anasazi. The Basketmakers did not have pottery and were not committed to intensive agriculture. They did possess a primitive type of corn, along with squash, both of which had come from Mexico. But they had not yet settled down to a fully sedentary life of tending fields and storing surplus crops.

As Wetherill and others noted, their beautiful and functional baskets were the Basketmakers' finest work. Baskets waterproofed with pine pitch could hold water; others were used as winnowing trays; and some served as cooking pots. Stone-lined storage and burial cists and shallow, saucer-shaped pithouses were about the only formal architecture of this time. The earliest examples of such homes, 1,500 to 2,000 years old, are at the Falls Creek rock shelters near Durango, Colorado. A fantastic array of perishable items, including jewelry, woven goods, and "mummies," was also found at the Falls Creek site.

Basketmaker tools included manos and metates, used to grind corn and other seeds. The mano was the stone held in the hand, and the metate was the flat rock on which the grains were crushed. Rather than bows and arrows, early Basketmakers hunted with atlatls, throwing sticks attached to their spears. With this extra propulsion, they increased the range of their weapons.

Manos and metates

Around A.D. 450 the Anasazi began to become more sedentary. They now possessed improved varieties of corn better suited to the Four Corners' shorter growing season, and beans were added to their list of cultivated crops. As they turned more attention to agriculture, a period called "Modified" Basketmaker ensued.

This period is also marked by a major innovation: the manufacture of pottery. Some believe the simultaneous arrival of beans and pottery is no coincidence: the longer cooking time required by beans demanded a sturdier vessel. The origin of pottery making among the Anasazi remains obscure; but the idea, or the pots themselves, likely first came up from the south, from the Mogollon people. Another innovation, the introduction of the bow and arrow, changed their lives as dramatically as did the use of pottery.

Still another monumental change during this period was the development of true pithouses that were strikingly similar in design and construction throughout the Four Corners. Usually circular, sometimes rectangular, these single-room dwellings were dug two to five feet deep using little more than sticks and handhewn wooden shovels. A smaller room was attached on the south or southeast side of some pithouses, a slab-lined or adobe-collared firepit was placed in the center of the main floor, and four upright posts supported the heavy roof beams. To enter and exit, people likely climbed up and down ladders that extended through a hole in the roof.

All of these developments were the germinating seeds for the next major Anasazi period—the Pueblo—which lasted from around A.D. 750 to 1450.

Evolution of Basketmaker pithouse to underground kiva and above ground dwelling over 600 years, approximately 550 AD to 1150 AD

THE PUEBLOS

The word "pueblo" has several meanings, referring to a time period, a style of building, and a people. The time period takes its name from the fact that around A.D. 700 to 750 the Anasazi began to build above-ground structures of several adjoining rooms. The Spaniards called these villages "pueblos" when they first saw them in the Southwest in the mid-1500s. The people who built and lived in them are called the Pueblos.

The rooms of pueblos were first built using a mud and stick construction called jacal (ha-call), or wattle and daub. A lattice of poles and sticks (wattle) was held together with mud (daub). The pueblo usually formed an arc, almost always opening to the southeast around a central plaza. Later pueblos consisted of rooms built of rock masonry, joined together into roomblocks standing one or more stories high. Living rooms were in the front, storage rooms in the back. Initially, each pueblo housed perhaps eight or ten families; but as the Pueblo period progressed, some were eventually expanded to hundreds of rooms sheltering hundreds of people.

Wattle and daub construction

Enclosed within the arc of almost every pueblo was a single pithouse that in time assumed great importance to the Anasazi. In early Pueblo times, the people continued to live in these structures and use them for storage or work places. As time passed, however, these central pithouses stopped being used as dwellings and became ceremonial spaces, or kivas, a word borrowed from the modern Pueblos for the structures in which they hold special ceremonies. Exactly when the evolution from dwelling to sacred place actually occurred is a subject of great debate among archeologists.

Several features distinguish kivas. These include a firepit with deflector and ventilator, a bench surrounding the inside of the room, and a hole in the floor, called the *sipapu*, the entryway into this world from below. Men of the clans likely gathered in the kivas for ceremonies; and in some pueblos the kiva was also the home of young men before they were married.

Cutaway showing components of kiva interior

Though the everyday smaller kivas persisted at some places larger ones, called "great kivas," were built. These circular, masonry-lined, partly below-ground structures were community centers of sorts, places where families of the community, or even people from outlying areas, could participate together in various activities. Here, during ceremonies, costumed dancers may have entered down ladders through a hole in the rooftop, chanting and beating drums in the kiva throughout the night. Casa Rinconada at Chaco Canyon, sixty-four feet in diameter, is an impressive example of this sort of structure, as is the great kiva at Aztec Ruins.

Backcountry kiva with original roof

During the earliest part of the Pueblo period, the Anasazi moved to higher elevations and to more northern climes, occupying the piñon-juniper forests at 5,000 to 6,000 feet, where staple foods such as piñon nuts were plentiful. Indeed, throughout Pueblo times the Anasazi did not hesitate to move from lower to higher and back to lower elevations, occupying new sites and reoccupying former ones as conditions warranted. This flexibility undoubtedly was the key to their survival—and success—in the tough and unpredictable land of the Four Corners.

Corrugated pottery

As with their architecture, Anasazi pottery also evolved during Pueblo times. From the earliest simple gray wares, the Pueblo peoples were soon making pots decorated with textured corrugations and black and white painted designs. An Anasazi potter built pots by winding coils of clay on top of each other, then smoothing those coils with a stone. Geometric designs were applied with black paint derived either from a mineral or from a plant such as boiled beeweed. Ceramics took myriad forms—bowls, jugs, mugs, plates, canteens, seed jars, and ollas.

Throughout the Pueblo period, the Four Corners Anasazi seemed to share ideas about what pottery should be.

Despite being spread over a huge geographic area, potters were faithful to uniform designs and to the coil-and-scrape method of construction. Besides its obvious utility, pottery served important functions as items of trade and as offerings to the dead.

Though Anasazi throughout the Four Corners had much in common, differences emerged as the society became more complex. These differences are seen most readily in masonry and kiva styles and village form and size, and somewhat in ceramics and other artifacts. The three major traditional "branches" of Anasazi in the Four Corners proper are Chaco Canyon, Kayenta, and Northern San Juan (or Mesa Verde). Sub-branches outside the Four Corners include the Virgin Anasazi in western Arizona and southwest Utah, the Rio Grande in north-central New Mexico, and the Little Colorado Anasazi to the south.

While the three branches provide a convenient organizational framework, it should be noted that there was a good deal of overlap among them. It is not unusual to find Chaco and Mesa Verde architecture side by side in the same site, and the same is true for Mesa Verde and Kayenta traits.

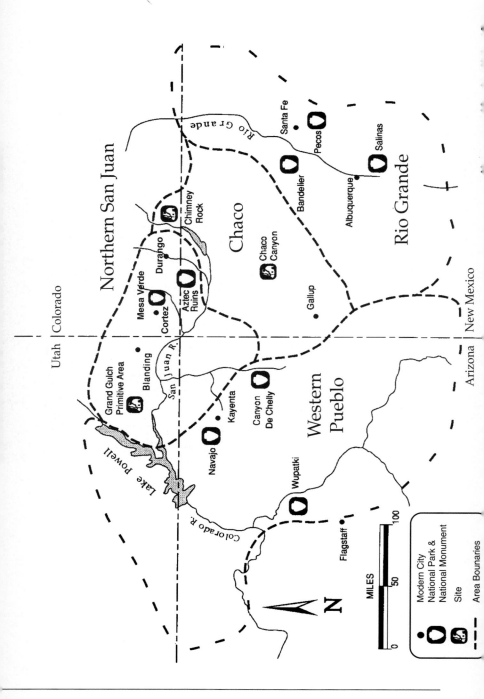

CHACO CANYON

Fajada Butte

In this dry canyon in northern New Mexico the "urban" expression of Anasazi culture first reached its peak from A.D. 900 to 1130. As archeologists Robert and Florence Lister wrote of the Chaco people, "They continued to be Anasazi, but a very special sort."

For anyone interested in the Anasazi, a visit to the remote, stunning sites in Chaco is a pilgrimage of sorts. The names of the ruins of Pueblo Bonito, Chetro Ketl, and Penasco Blanco are spoken almost with reverence. These and six other "great houses" of several hundred rooms grew up along the north side of Chaco Wash. Their masonry is unsurpassed in the Four Corners; some say, in the world. Chacoan stoneworkers carefully dressed sandstone slabs and laid them up in walls, some four and five stories high. Smaller stones were used as chinking to create a beautiful banded veneer pattern. The inner core of the walls was rock rubble.

Chaco masonry

The people of Chaco also employed several ingenious techniques to capture and control water. During even minor rainstorms, water cascades off the bedrock cliffs behind Chaco Wash. Chacoan farmers built small earthen dams at the base of these cliffs to capture this runoff in reservoirs. Canals tapping into the reservoirs then carried water to grids of gardens and fields planted along the wash. A dense concentration of such features has been documented in the central section of Chaco Wash.

In addition to constructing fine pueblos and clever irrigation systems, Chacoans spent a great deal of time building roads, a curious undertaking given that they possessed neither wheels nor beasts of burden. Aerial photos have revealed evidence of an estimated 300 miles of roads. These straight, well-engineered paths, bermed on the shoulders and averaging thirty feet wide, radiate out at least fifty to sixty miles in several directions from Chaco. The roadbuilders let little stand in their way, pushing up and over hills and through washes. Chacoan roads are still being discovered, connecting with outliers, such as Pueblo Pintado to the east and Casamero to the south, that also have great houses and other Chacoan features.

Building the roads, water works, and great houses undoubtedly required huge amounts of material and labor. But not all of life at Chaco was heavy manual labor. Some Chacoans possessed and traded special luxury items, including obsidian, exquisite jewelry of imported shell and turquoise, carved and painted wooden ceremonial items, and feathers from Mexican parrots.

These goods, along with the fantastic architecture, road system, and large number of great kivas, all point to Chaco as an important center of Anasazi culture. The "Chaco Phenomenon," as it's called, may have functioned as a food redistribution system, with people from the outliers toting in baskets of corn and dried meat to supply the elite who lived in the great houses in

Copper bell trade item

Chaco Canyon. Others see these pilgrims coming to the center as part of a far-flung ritual and ceremonial network.

Strong though it appears to have been, the Chaco Phenomenon began to wane by the mid-1100s. By 1130 almost no new construction was occurring in Chaco Canyon. A combination of severe drought from 1130 to 1190, alkali-crusted soils, and depleted timber and game animals may have contributed to the final irreparable tear in the elaborate social fabric of Chaco. By the early 1200s, the Anasazi's 700-year occupation of Chaco Canyon had ended.

Serpentine stone pipe

NORTHERN SAN JUAN

Cliff Palace

At some Chaco outlier towns, such as Lowry Pueblo in southwest Colorado, two types of masonry walls abut one another. One style is distinctly Chacoan, while the other is Mesa Verdean. Using the two adjoining styles of masonry as a clue, it appears that people from both the Northern San Juan and Chaco areas lived at Lowry at various times.

Mesa Verde itself, the prominent highland overlooking the Montezuma and Mancos valleys in southwest Colorado, is considered by many to epitomize this part of the Anasazi world. The classic view of Cliff Palace from the overlook in Mesa Verde National Park embodies the image of the Anasazi for many people.

But research in Montezuma Valley in particular has shown that the stunning cliff dwellings of Mesa Verde tell only part of the story of a larger regional variation now called the Northern San Juan Anasazi. This subregion includes a substantial area north of the San Juan River, from the Abajo Mountains and Comb Ridge in southeast Utah into the valleys of Montezuma Creek, and the Mancos, Animas, and Piedra rivers east of Durango, Colorado.

Comb Ridge and Abajo Mountains

The Northern San Juan people followed the standard Anasazi path, moving from pithouses to above-ground, open pueblos. Small Basketmaker pithouse villages had been established on Mesa Verde and in Montezuma Valley by A.D. 600. Grandparents, parents, and children probably all lived together in the tight confines of a single pithouse. And they were already making pottery and growing the three main crops—corn, beans, and squash.

By the 800s classic pueblo style architecture had emerged among the Northern San Juan groups. Clusters of these pueblos adjoined to form larger villages, as seen at Mesa Verde, on Alkali Ridge east of Blanding, and in Montezuma Valley. The first of these pueblos were wattle and daub, but by the 900s the builders were incorporating sandstone masonry, giving more permanence to their homes. Kivas in the Northern San Juan pueblos all seem to have followed the same blueprint. They were uniformly built below ground and typically were keyhole shaped because of the addition of a small room on the south or southeast side.

By the 1100s, people had joined together to form the huge towns of Lowry and Yellowjacket in Montezuma Valley, and Farview on Mesa Verde. Lowry and Yellowjacket, along with a half dozen others, may have served as centers for surrounding rural villages. These big towns had a remarkable infrastructure, with streets, great kivas, and artificial reservoirs to serve hundreds, perhaps even a few thousand, residents.

Not until A.D. 1200 did the residents of Mesa Verde turn to the sweeping cliff alcoves to construct the now famous dwellings such as Square Tower House, Balcony House, Spruce Tree House, and Long House, along with lesser-

Eagles Nest, Ute Mountain Tribal Park

known ones in canyons on the Ute Mountain Reservation just south of Mesa Verde. Though their homes were now below the mesa, Anasazi farmers still went back and forth frequently to tend their mesa-top fields.

The people in the hinterlands, at places like nearby Hovenweep, were building elegant multistory towers at this time. These enigmatic structures, often found at the heads of canyons, may have functioned as astronomical observatories, watchtowers, or as great silos to store grain.

If the Chacoans were the elite among the Anasazi, the Northern San Juan Anasazi were the working folk. Their lives were in many respects utilitarian. They manufactured quality tools—bone awls, flint knives, and stone hoes—with which they could make clothes, build homes, and grow food. Their masonry was thick and sturdy, single or double courses of blocky sandstone, finely done but not as delicate as that of the Chacoan pueblos.

The Northern San Juan Anasazi wove good baskets of yucca and willow, along with blankets of turkey feathers and rabbit fur to keep them warm during the cold winters. Anthropologist Richard W. Lang has said that to them, "A field of cactus, yucca and grasses was not a barren place, but a storehouse and a garden that would. . . yield fiber for cordage, footwear, baskets, and more." The mule deer so plentiful among the oak groves on Mesa Verde would have been prime prey for Northern San Juan hunters, and the resources of the San Juan Mountains were not far away.

The pottery of this group is especially admired. The earliest Anasazi in the region possessed the potter's skill. They quarried the raw material from the clay-rich Mancos Shale and fired the pots in the absence of oxygen to obtain their gray color. The best pottery is called Mesa Verde Black-on-white, a style marked by bold abstract designs on a polished pearly white surface. In contrast, Chacoan pottery designs were more angular, with fine hatching on a chalky white surface.

Chacoan style pottery design

Mesa Verde style pottery design

Kayenta style pottery design

In their higher, wetter country the Northern San Juan people encouraged greater abundance from the soil. The region has been called the "breadbasket" of the Anasazi, and the surplus crops they produced there likely were traded with people in other parts of the Four Corners.

Despite their environmental advantages, the Northern San Juan Anasazi met the same fate as the Chacoans had earlier. Around A.D. 1300, only a century after the famous cliff dwellings in the Mesa Verde area were built, the region was abandoned. The people are believed to have moved, as did the Chacoans, to the better watered Hopi, Zuni, and Rio Grande areas. Many of the same reasons have been suggested for abandonment of the Northern San Juan area as for Chaco Canyon; the true explanation may be a combination of these.

Archeologist Linda Cordell theorizes that small bands of people, in family and kin groups, left first. Seeing their friends and neighbors leave, the others decided to follow. Her guess is that, "weighed against human fellowship and a rich and secure social life, the quiet canyons and mesas would lose every time."

KAYENTA

Betatakin, Navajo National Monument

The third major Four Corners Anasazi branch was centered in the maze of slickrock known as the Tsegi Canyon system, near the town of Kayenta in northeast Arizona. The homeland of the Kayenta Anasazi also included the huge area south and west of Comb Ridge in southeast Utah, and Black Mesa, and stretched all the way south and west into the Grand Canyon and Wupatki area.

The Kayenta Anasazi have been characterized as bohemian, backwater bumpkins compared to their more citified cousins, the Northern San Juan and Chaco Anasazi. But a look at the gorgeous cliff dwellings of Betatakin or Keet Seel in Navajo National Monument, and at their fine pottery, quickly dispels this notion.

The general traits shared by Anasazi throughout the Four Corners, were there: the Kayentans made pottery, built masonry pueblos, and grew corn. But they also exhibited several attributes unique to them. Instead of joining together into large towns, they lived primarily in smaller family groups. Some Kayenta Anasazi continued to live in pithouses, even as their neighbors were choosing the pueblo style of housing. Neither did they build great kivas; and their smaller village kivas were sometimes rectangular, a departure from the round kivas found throughout the rest of Anasazi territory. Kayentans made some of the finest pottery in the Southwest, including distinctive black-on-whites, along with exquisite polished orange and red wares.

The rock work of Kayentan pueblos was of a chunky, unpatterned style, completed by the addition of copious amounts of mortar to hold the roughly hewn stone blocks in place. They also used a striking wattle and daub technique, weaving willow and yucca splints together and plastering this latticework with mud.

Although they continued to use the same building materials and techniques, after A.D. 1250 the Kayentans began to relocate their homes in sandstone alcoves in the Tsegi system and in Canyon de Chelly.

Keet Seel

Though they had used these shelters throughout most of the centuries here, this is when they began to build what the Navajos call *tse yaa kin*," houses beneath the rocks," the most famous of which are Betatakin and Keet Seel. So well camouflaged were these structures that intruders would have had trouble finding them. The Kayenta Anasazi may also have taken to the canyon walls to house growing numbers of people or to free up needed farmland along the canyon bottoms.

As at Mesa Verde, the cliff-dwelling period marked the end of the occupation of Kayenta land. The latest of these pueblos dates from the middle 1280s, after which time the Kayenta people left the region, probably completely by A.D. 1300. A major period of arroyo-cutting may have caused the water table to drop and eaten away the Kayentans' farmlands. Such climatic forces, along with possible depletion of fuelwood or other resources resulting from the Kayentans' own actions, may have forced the emigration. Invasion by enemies, specifically the Utes and Paiutes, has been proposed as well.

Though we don't know precisely why they left, at least we have a good idea where they went. By A.D. 1300 the town of Old Oraibi on Third Mesa had been occupied for two hundred years. It was to this mesa, sixty miles to the southwest, and to First and Second mesas at Hopi, that the Kayenta people probably went.

By the 1300s the Anasazi had left the Four Corners. Four basic explanations for the abandonment have been debated: drought, especially the so-called "great drought" between A.D. 1276 and 1299; arroyo-cutting and consequent dropping of the water table and loss of tillable land; diseases of epidemic proportions; and warfare. Others have proposed that perhaps it was simply the age-old attraction of the "bright lights" that lured the people to the major population centers. But why they all left, and why they never returned, are questions that still stir vigorous discussion among archeologists and nonarcheologists alike.

One of those centers of population was the Rio Grande Valley in northern New Mexico. Bandelier National Monument, about forty-five miles north of Santa Fe, provides a good view of an important prehistoric Rio Grande refuge for Four Corners Anasazi. In the honeycomb cavities of the volcanic tuff of the Pajarito Plateau and along lush Frijoles Creek, the Anasazi found new places to rebuild their homes and farms from the 1200s into the 1500s, when the Spaniards arrived.

Ceremonial Cave, Bandelier National Monument

A walk along the Ruins Trail in Frijoles Canyon in Bandelier leads to the circular pueblo called Tyuonyi. A half mile farther up the canyon are Long House and Ceremonial Cave. On a mesa in a small outlying section of the park are the hidden walls of another pueblo, Tsankawi. The sacred Shrine of the Stone Lions near a site called Yapashi is still visited by Native Americans, especially

Bandelier

people from Cochiti Pueblo. Like their Anasazi ancestors, the modern-day inhabitants of Cochiti and the other Rio Grande Pueblos have chosen to live where there is water to support them and their crops.

Water. Always water. The great determiner of life in the Four Corners country. Above all else, the Anasazi must have been geniuses when it came to finding water. Wandering today among their canyon homes, at any time other than the summer monsoons, we find streambeds filled with nothing but dry sand, cracked mud, and bare rock. The plants are shrunken and barbed. Only a lone cottonwood, outrageously green in the dun-colored land, says water may be present. No doubt their eyes feasted on these green oases as much as ours do today.

Once again the question arises, "How did the Anasazi do it?" The answers reveal that they must have been a tough, enduring people, who possessed an admirable adaptability and cleverness.

Rio Grande style orge

THE SITES

Beef Basin

In the summer of 1990, the Anasazi Heritage Center in Dolores, Colorado hosted the Four Corners Governors' Conference. Recognizing the rich cultural resources of the Four Corners, conference participants sought to develop a collective vision for the region and those resources. Working groups reported on ways to break down institutional barriers between states, tribes, and governmental agencies; to educate and involve the public; and to protect the region's world-class archeological sites. To these ends, they agreed to establish a Four Corners Heritage Council, and the San Juan National Forest Association set out to publish a guidebook to Four Corners archeological sites and modern Indian reservations.

Cavate room, Bandelier National Monument

Ruin in the Sand Canyon Archeological Area, Sleeping Ute Mountain in the distance

Escalante Ruins located on a hill above the Anasazi Heritage Center, the Mesa Verde on the horizon

Keet Seel National Monument

Hovenweep Castle located at the head of Square Tower Canyon, Hovenweep National Monument

River House on the San Juan River

Spider Rock, Canyon de Chelly

Pueblo Bonito interior

There are literally thousands of Anasazi sites on public, private, and tribal lands in the Four Corners; thus a selection necessarily had to be made to keep this guidebook to a reasonable length. The fifty or so sites listed here meet the general criteria of being safe and open to the public for at least three months of the year, having interpretive information available, and being managed primarily on a noncommercial basis. Most contain prehistoric remains, though modern Indian reservations, museums devoted to archeological or Native American themes, and nonprofit educational centers and groups are also included. Descriptions of the sites are accompanied by directions, access and fee information, and administrative contacts.

The list and the text reflect an implicit hierarchy of sites. The first tier, and most detailed, includes the crown jewels of archeology in America's national park system—Mesa Verde National Park, Chaco Culture National Historical Park, and Canyon de Chelly National Monument. The second tier consists of those sites not as well known but still fairly easily reached by paved roads, or in a few cases by graded gravel roads. These are managed under various governmental and tribal jurisdictions. The third category includes "backcountry" sites—those accessible primarily by four-wheel-drive, on foot, or by boat. The information provided for these is purposefully the least

Backcountry site

detailed; visitors are advised to contact local offices of the administering agency or tribe for specifics on accessibility and any necessary permits.

Visitors should be forewarned that they may find some administrators hesitant to dispense much information about backcountry sites because many of these sites are fragile and vulnerable to vandalism. Illegal pothunting and defacing of rock art in archeological sites has reached epidemic proportions in the Southwest, and law enforcement alone cannot solve the problem. Add to this the impact of legitimate use—the sheer weight of too many footsteps on delicate walls and soils—and the wariness about publicizing the sites becomes understandable. There are, however, rules of etiquette and ethics that visitors to all sites should observe to lessen that impact to protect these irreplaceable resources.

Fragile walls of ruins in Arch Canyon

ETIQUETTE

All artifacts, structures, and rock art are protected by federal law. It is not only unethical, but illegal to remove any pottery sherds, stones, woven goods, or other items from public lands. Artifacts provide one of the main ways of dating sites. More important, when artifacts are removed from their prehistoric resting places their context is lost. For archeologists it is like finding an item in a kitchen that belonged in a bathroom. The value and meaning of the item are nearly lost. Be content to record your "finds" on film and resist the urge to lay out neat displays of artifacts on rocks at sites.

Do not climb, walk, lean, or sit on the walls or roofs of any structure. The mortar, plaster, and adobe are, in many cases, a thousand years old and they are fragile. Again, valuable information is lost if the walls are collapsed.

Trash heaps (called middens) left by prehistoric occupants are another source of information. The middens are soft mounds that accumulated usually in front of and downhill from pueblos. They consist of layers of pottery sherds and organic debris that accumulated over the years a site was occupied. That layering can be deciphered only if it has not been disturbed. Avoid walking on middens, and never dig or in any way mix their contents.

Rock art—pictographs and petroglyphs—likewise

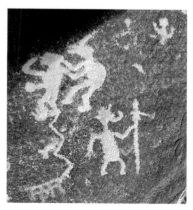

Galisteo Basin petroglyphs

should not be touched; nor should rubbings of them be made. Oils on hands and fingers can damage the drawings.

Common courtesy should be observed when visiting modern Indian reservations. The best advice is simply to remain as unobtrusive as possible and act as you would wish someone to act in your home. Photographing, sketching, and recording are prohibited on some reservations, and where allowed should never be done without permission. Inquire at tribal centers about visiting villages or other parts of reservations and about attending any ceremonies.

ADVICE FOR TRAVELERS

The Four Corners is *big* country, a fact which imposes special demands on travelers. Distances are great and towns are small, which means services like automobile repair and medical help simply may not be available within fifty or even a hundred miles. Likewise, facilities and accommodations at sites listed in this book vary from highly developed to completely undeveloped. Local inquiry and advance reservations may be necessary, especially during the busy summer and fall travel seasons.

Weather is a major consideration for travelers in this region, due primarily to its outstanding unpredictableness. Spring and autumn, the best times to travel in the Four Corners, are seasons of sudden changes. On an April day, you may be walking comfortably in shirt sleeves one moment, and an hour later have to put on a down jacket, hat, and gloves.

Summer is the monsoon season. Strong thunderstorms, with torrential rains and lightning, occur in the afternoons during July and August. Often extremely local, these downpours give rise to flashflooding. Low spots in roads can become impassable for a time, and normally dry streambeds can fill bank to bank in a matter of minutes. High winds accompany storm systems, and are especially notorious in the changeable spring. Strong crosswinds can threaten high-profile vehicles.

A few major paved roads cross the Four Corners country; the rest are unpaved back roads in various states of repair from good graded gravel, to deep sand, to unnegotiable wet mud. Four-wheel-drive is helpful (though some local wags say it just gets you stuck deeper). Any backroad touring requires that you take along a

shovel, extra food and water, and a sleeping bag during most of the year. Inquire locally about road conditions, especially if you plan to go far off any paved road.

The Four Corners also contains a great deal of unfenced grazing land. Drivers should always be aware of the possibility of sheep, cattle, or horses being on the roads. This caution applies especially at night, when deer may also unexpectedly dash onto the road.

For those adequately prepared, a journey in the dramatic and startlingly beautiful Four Corners area will never be forgotten.

Island in the Sky District, Canyonlands

CHACO

Chaco Canyon

CHACO CULTURE NATIONAL HISTORICAL PARK

A local Four Corners newspaper declares that Chaco Canyon is for the "cerebral tourist." Why this is so is not readily apparent from the article, but the implication is that the deeper archeologists and visitors delve into this showplace of Southwest archeology, the more absorbing questions they unearth.

Indeed, as you jolt along on the twenty to thirty miles of washboard roads leading into Chaco Canyon, you may ask your own questions. For example, why did the Anasazi choose this location to display their greatest building and engineering efforts? After seeing the soaring walls of Pueblo Bonito and the exquisite masonry of the great kiva at Casa Rinconada, you may ask what motivated them to invest such extraordinary amounts of time and labor? As archeologists Robert and Florence Lister wrote: "More impressive than the massive ruins themselves is the evident force of the human spirit that was responsible for their erection." And in the face of such an impressive investment, what could have forced them to leave it all behind?

These are some of the major puzzles surrounding the prehistoric dwellers of Chaco Canyon—and what has become known as the "Chaco Phenomenon." Here in this lonely, dry canyon in what is now northern New Mexico, with an average rainfall of only about nine inches a year, the Anasazi built and lived in what amounted to, for their culture, major urban areas. They built an entire road system to connect with outlying communities and engineered structures to irrigate their fields of corn, squash, and beans. They made beautiful black and white pottery, and somehow acquired luxury goods like turquoise, obsidian, and copper bells, from places far distant from Chaco Canyon.

Richard Wetherill, of Mesa Verde fame, also pioneered archeological work at Chaco. Guiding a Kansas farm family through the Southwest, he first arrived at Chaco in the fall of 1895. (The daughter of the family, Marietta Palmer, would become Richard's bride a year later.) They camped at Pueblo Bonito, and proceeded to explore Chaco for a month, digging here and there, then finally packing up their belongings as the gray skies of November closed in over the canyon.

A gathering of Navajos around the Wetherill house at Pueblo Bonito
From Richard Wetherill: Anasazi, *book by Frank McNitt*

After describing to his wealthy benefactor Talbot Hyde the abundant relics to be had at Chaco, Richard secured necessary financial backing. For the next four years, he worked in Chaco. His first task was an excavation of Pueblo Bonito, where he dug into the trash mounds in front of the pueblo. Surprisingly few burials, with an accompanying lack of valuable grave goods, were found. Ensuing seasons at Pueblo Bonito proved far more productive, with 114 cylinder vessels found along with a quiver filled with arrows, carved wooden staffs, flutes, stone effigies, and a hoard of turquoise jewelry.

Richard Wetherill did not just make archeological observations. He also noticed that the local Navajos had to journey a great distance for supplies. His obvious solution was to build a trading post at Chaco Canyon. The post was tacked onto the north wall of Pueblo Bonito, built of the rock and wood from the Anasazi ruins; and from the beginning it proved a smart business venture.

A host of East Coast archeologists were visiting Chaco Canyon by this time. All were intrigued, though some were disturbed by what they considered the uncontrolled removal of artifacts. Their concern, along with that of Gustaf Nordenskiöld, who was working at Mesa Verde at the time, manifested itself in passage of the Antiquities Act in 1906. In the act, Congress declared it illegal to

appropriate, excavate, or damage any historic or prehistoric ruins or objects on public lands of the United States. In a related move, President Theodore Roosevelt designated eighteen areas as national monuments. Chaco Canyon was among them.

The story that has emerged from all this attention is one of a flourishing culture. Indeed many see Chaco as the highest expression of the Anasazi culture. Between A.D. 900 to 1115 the Anasazi built nine multistoried "great houses" at Chaco—Hungo Pavi, Chetro Ketl, Pueblo Bonito, Pueblo Alto, Pueblo del Arroyo, and others. Each of these huge, well-planned buildings contains from 200 to 700 rooms and several kivas. All are easily accessible along the Ruins Loop Road or within short walking distance.

The Cliffhouse Sandstone of the canyon walls provided the rock for the Chacoans' expert masonry. Their distinctive, stylized masonry was perhaps the best known to prehistory. Great care was taken to dress boulders, which were laid into place and secured by many smaller pieces of stone chinking in intricate patterns. At Chetro Ketl alone, an estimated 50 million pieces of sandstone were used. Enormous amounts of other material were also required—some 215,000 trees were cut and brought in for the beams of the great house floors and roofs.

Chetro Ketl

Recent research has shown that only about a hundred people may actually have lived in each of the great houses—casting doubt on early population figures estimating as many as 5,000 people at Chaco. Lack of evidence for living rooms, lack of burials, and limited amount of cultivatable land at Chaco have cast doubt on such high figures. Some archeologists, however, think the Chacoans' resourceful control of water could have supported that many people.

In the 1970s, applying aerial and remote-sensing techniques, archeologists studied the roads emanating from Chaco Canyon. These straight, broad footpaths—thirty feet wide in places, some marked by shrines and signal towers—extend like spokes from the hub. As studies of the road system continue, its true extent is becoming known. Some of the roads may reach as far north as the San Juan Mountains in Colorado and as far south as the Mogollon Mountains in southwest New Mexico.

Another intriguing find has been the identification of outlying sites along these roads, perhaps as many as 120 of them in the 26,000-square-mile San Juan Basin. An "outlier" is a community consisting of a central large house surrounded by a cluster of smaller residential buildings. The multistory central building exhibits Chaco-style masonry and has large rooms laid out in a formal plan. At least one kiva is enclosed within the block of rooms, and a great kiva is usually associated with the site. A road usually connects with the site as well.

What was the purpose of the roads and these so-called outliers? Trade is the currently favored hypothesis. The great houses of Chaco may have functioned as centers of an extensive regional distribution network, in which goods like turquoise, salt, copper bells, macaw feathers, chipped stone, pottery, and food were imported and exported.

*Petroglyph of parrot -
knowledge of these birds indicates
trade with Mesoamerica*

But by A.D. 1130, nearly all construction had ceased at Chaco Canyon. The elaborate system appeared to have collapsed. Why, we do not know; but a few theories have been proposed, including a shift in the center of power to Casas Grandes in Mexico, unfavorable environmental conditions, and a society that collapsed under its own complexity.

After a stop at the visitor center, you may wish to drive along the seven-mile, one-way Ruins Loop to see several major Chaco sites. Short trails, with trail leaflets, lead through Pueblo Bonito, Chetro Ketl, Una Vida, Casa Rinconada, and Pueblo del Arroyo. You may walk three to six miles to see others, including the Pueblo Alto complex with its impressive view of the San Juan Basin and strategic location as the origin and terminus of many Chacoan roads. Wijiji, Casa Chiquita, Penasco Blanco, and Tsin Kletsin also can be reached by short hikes. Visitors must remain on designated trails in the park.

LOCATION: 70 miles South of Farmington, New Mexico. ACCESS: From New Mexico 26 at Nageezi, follow Highway 57 for 30 unpaved miles. From Thoreau, follow NM 371 for 44 miles, then turn north onto NM 57 for a very rough 21 miles. Both entry roads are passable to passenger vehicles, but travel during wet weather is risky.

CONTACT: Superintendent
Chaco Culture National Historical Park
Star Route 4, Box 6500
Bloomfield, NM 87413
(505) 988-6727

Pueblo Bonito

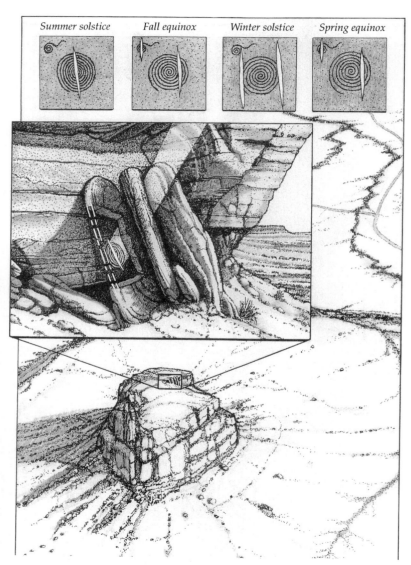

Summer solstice   Fall equinox   Winter solstice   Spring equinox

"Sun Dagger" on Fajada Butte -- insert shows three boulders (one with cutout)
through which the angles of the sun mark the seasons solstices and equinox

Casa del Arroyo, Chaco Canyon

Sunrise at Pueblo Bonito. Pieces of what was known as Threatening Rock lie in the foreground. In 1941 a large section of Disconnected Cliff collapsed onto the northeast corner of Pueblo Bonito destroying sixty-five rooms.

Pueblo Bonito, Chaco Culture National Historical Park

Great Kiva, Aztec National Monument

Cottonwoods, Aztec National Monument

Sunset on East Kiva, Chimney Rock Archaeological Area

Overview of Chimney Rock Pueblo, Chimney Rock Archaeological Area

Lowry Pueblo

AZTEC RUINS
NATIONAL MONUMENT

Great Kiva, Aztec Ruins

Entering the great kiva at Aztec can be a religious experience for some. This cavernous circular structure, the only
one of its kind fully restored in the Southwest, may be the
closest thing to a prehistoric church that we will ever
know.

Aztec Ruins is famous for its great kiva, excavated and reconstructed by Earl Morris between 1921 and 1934. Morris, born and raised near these ruins on the Animas River in northwest New Mexico, was hired by the American Museum of Natural History to excavate Aztec. One of his major tasks was to rebuild the great kiva, which was to him "the most intricate sort of sanctuary that was ever developed by the Pueblo people."

Nearly fifty feet in diameter, Aztec's great kiva is one of the largest known. Four massive pillars of mortar and wood supported the roof, which weighed about ninety-five tons. The pillars rested on gigantic discs of limestone brought in from fifty miles away. If we use our imaginations, we can hear the rhythmic pounding of the foot drums and the soothing repetition of the chants, and smell the piñon smoke wafting up from the fire that burns all night.

The size of great kivas, and the number of people they likely accommodated, reinforces the notion that these were public places. Not only ceremonies, but governmental meetings and social events might also have been held in them.

Entrance into the great kiva is the culmination of a visit to the West Ruins at Aztec, the portion of the site open to the public. But even if the great kiva were not there, this would be an impressive pueblo. Earl Morris was also responsible for clearing and restoring most of the 400 rooms of the rectangular-shaped pueblo. Legend says that Earl's father, Scott Morris, sent his three-year-old son out to play in the sand on their farm, just down-

Earl Morris, from Among Ancient Ruins, *book by University of Colorado Museum*

stream from Aztec, and young Earl dug up a piece of pottery, thus launching his lifelong career in Southwestern archeology. Later, Earl and his wife, Ann, were to live in Aztec, and their home is now part of the visitor center and museum.

The 400-yard trail that begins just outside the visitor center follows along the back wall of the pueblo. The innovative prehistoric masons at Aztec added a few courses of green stone across the 360-foot length of this wall, in contrast with the large golden sandstone blocks that make up the rest of the walls.

So well-preserved are the rooms of this pueblo that one man remarked, "It gives me chills every time I come through here." You must duck your head as you pass through the small doorways, and once within the cool stone rooms you can still see the original ponderosa, cottonwood, and juniper beams in the ceilings. Samples taken from the ponderosa beams have been used to date the construction of Aztec at around A.D. 1110.

Either Aztec's first inhabitants migrated in from Chaco Canyon, or the locals so liked what they saw of their big-city neighbors that they adopted their techniques. Aztec is counted as one of four major Chacoan-style villages, and in size it nearly equalled Pueblo Bonito or Chetro Ketl. With good farmland, plentiful water, and available wood, farmers here had everything they needed for a healthy subsistence life.

But they left Aztec after only about five generations, around the same time the Chacoan system collapsed. Then, during the 1200s, groups with ties to Mesa Verde moved down, remodeled, and lived at the site. By 1300, following twenty very dry years, Aztec was abandoned for good. The residents perhaps moved east to the Rio Grande pueblos or to the Hopi Mesas in Arizona.

The self-guided trail through the Aztec ruin also leads to one of only a handful of examples of a curious feature among Southwest sites: triwall structures. Three concentric walls encircle what is believed to be a kiva. The one at Aztec is named the Hubbard Site, for an early settler. It was excavated by the National Park Service in 1953 and backfilled in 1979 for protection.

LOCATION: On Highway 550, 14 miles east of Farmington. ACCESS: In Aztec, turn north off Highway 550 and go one-half mile on Ruins Road to the visitor center. FEE: Yes

CONTACT: Superintendent
             P.O. Box 640
             Aztec, NM 87410
             (505) 334-6174

SALMON RUINS

Just down the road from Aztec sits another large Chacoan-style village. Salmon Ruins, administered by the San Juan County (NM) Museum Association, is an impressive site that underwent major excavation in the late 1960s.

Hoosier homesteader Pete Salmon, for whom the site is named, had protected the ruins on his land during the early part of the century. But by the 1960s the property was on the market, to be subdivided and sold to prospective pothunters. Museum Association members rescued Salmon in 1969, raising enough money to buy the site and then seeing that an archeologist was hired to excavate it. By that time, the site had been fairly surrounded by housing and industrial development associated with the towns of Farmington and Bloomfield.

Archeologist Cynthia Irwin-Williams of Eastern New Mexico University was employed to conduct the excavations. She had expected to find only about twenty to forty rooms. But upon inspection she was shocked to find a ruin nearly a city block long with 150 ground-floor rooms and 100 second-story rooms. Despite the daunting size of the task, work proceeded producing volumes of fascinating information about this pueblo community beside the San Juan River.

Tree-ring dates indicated that Salmon was built in only six years, beginning in A.D. 1088. The ponderosa, Douglas fir, and white fir beams that furnished the dates had been cut in the La Plata Mountains, seventy-five miles north in present-day Colorado, and brought in and stockpiled at Salmon.

Like neighboring Aztec, Salmon was connected to Chaco Canyon, forty-five miles away. Salmon sits at the end of a major Chacoan road, called the Great North Road. Also as at Aztec, Chacoan residents abandoned their home in A.D. 1150, and Mesa Verdeans moved in a century later.

Irwin-Williams believed that an elite group of specialists oversaw the lives of Salmon residents. They held authority over their constituent farmers, knew about cultivating corn and other advanced farming techniques, and likely were the ones who announced the times of the seasonal ceremonies around which pueblo life revolved. They also probably controlled activities in the unusual above-ground Tower Kiva, the great kiva, and other places in the community where important ceremonies were staged.

Though designed as a place of ceremony, Salmon's Tower Kiva turned out to be a place of tragedy. Around the year A.D. 1263, when Mesa Verdeans lived at Salmon, a fire started in the ceiling of a nearby room. To save them

Children's hand prints

from the flames, young children of the village were ush-
ered into the Tower Kiva. But the fire reached the Tower
Kiva, and its roof collapsed. Fifty or more children, all
under six years old, died. Their scorched skeletons were
unearthed during excavations, and many were found
holding one another in their arms. Shortly after this time,
the residents of Salmon abandoned their pueblo.

LOCATION: Highway 64, two miles west of Bloomfield, 13
miles east of Farmington, NM. ACCESS: Turn south off
Highway 64 at the sign. Large circular building is San Juan
County Archeological Research Center and Library. Entry
to ruins is through the Center, which exhibits a small
selection of the million and a half artifacts recovered
during the excavations. A trail guide also is available here.
The graveled trail that leads through the ruins begins
outside the Center. The adjoining Heritage Park contains
Pete Salmon's adobe house, circa 1901, along with recon-
structions of dwellings of modern-day southwestern
Indians. FEE: Yes

CONTACT: Director
             Salmon Ruin
             P.O. Box 125
             Bloomfield, NM 87413
             (505) 632-2013

CASAMERO

An astounding 120 communities have been identified as "outliers," part of the eleventh-century Chaco Phenomenon. When the system was at its height, many of these outliers were joined to the hub in Chaco Canyon in northern New Mexico by wide roads.

Casamero Ruin, 60 miles south of Chaco Canyon, is a good example of one of these outlier pueblos. It is only a few miles off Interstate 40, and contains a great house (the pueblo), great kiva, parts of two prehistoric roads, and several small houses. It sits at the base of a redrock mesa called Ojo Tecolote, or Owl Eye, for the two large alcoves in the cliff.

The influence of Chaco Canyon is most notable in the uniform architecture of the outlier pueblos. The masonry was excellent. Walls were often laid up with a rubble core, veneered with the flattest, finest shaped rocks. Ranks of rooms were arranged, often in an overall E, D, L, or U shape, around a central plaza that contained a kiva. The pueblos opened to the east or south, while solid back walls usually faced north and west. Chaco-style pottery, other fine crafts, and trade goods have also been found at out liers.

Though small in size, Casamero Pueblo shows the typically fine rock masonry of all Chaco-style buildings. Some of the chinking between the larger boulders includes bits of broken pottery. The federal Bureau of Land Management stabilized the knee-high walls of Casamero, so this open site remains well preserved.

In the late 1960s and early 1970s, archeologists found burned corncobs and turkey shell fragments in one room, and the burial of a small child in another. The great kiva, about 200 yards from the pueblo, is unexcavated.

LOCATION: 20 miles west of Grants, NM, off Interstate 40. ACCESS: At the small town of Prewitt, NM, turn north on Generating Station Road. Go 4 1/2 miles, mostly on paved road, to sign and parking area for Casamero. The ruin is within a short walking distance. FEE: No

CONTACT: Bureau of Land Management
             Farmington Resource Area
             1235 La Plata Highway
             Farmington, NM 87401
             (505) 599-8900

LOWRY PUEBLO

Eight hundred years ago Anasazi farmers found some ruins of *their* ancestors, and decided to rebuild at the same place. The structures we now see at Lowry Pueblo were built sometime between A.D. 1080 and the early 1100s, directly on top of an eighth-century pithouse village.

The excavated rooms of Lowry Pueblo were home to nearly a hundred people, who farmed and worshiped here near the head of Cow Canyon. For water in this dry country, they located a spring and built their own reservoir. The village was expanded several times. At its height between A.D. 1085 and 1170, this pueblo consisted of nearly seventy-five rooms, a great kiva, and a special kiva painted with murals. Though nearly 100 miles from Chaco Canyon, Lowry is considered by some to have been established originally as a Chaco outlier.

Like other Anasazi groups, Lowry's inhabitants made their living by farming corn, beans, squash, and tobacco. But a few unusual features hint that this may have been a special site. One is the forty-five-foot diameter great kiva where people from surrounding areas may have gathered for ceremonies. Another is the painted kiva (which visitors may enter). The mineral paints used on the kiva's wall mural deteriorated after the structure was open to the air during excavation, and what remains has crumbled nearly beyond recognition. Pieces of the original panel have been removed for study to the Anasazi Heritage Center in Dolores, Colorado.

The actual town of Lowry was much bigger than this single site suggests. As many as 1,800 people may have lived here, spread across a square mile of this part of the Montezuma Valley. Archeologists estimate that there were perhaps a hundred similar housing units organized around roads, plazas, and small kivas.

Ute Mountain, with its unmistakable profile, rises to the south, undoubtedly a significant landmark to the prehis-

View of Ute Mountain from Sand Canyon Archeological Area

toric residents. Lowry is one of those choice places just far enough off the beaten path that few people go there. It is a delightful place for a pleasant tour and Sunday picnic. A self-guided interpretive trail leads through the site.

LOCATION: 30 miles northwest of Cortez, CO, at Pleasant View. ACCESS: Take Highway 666 north from Cortez, turn west at Pleasant View on RD CC; the first four miles paved, last five miles, gravel. Though the pueblo is open year-round, the road is not maintained in winter. FEE: None.

CONTACT: Area Manager
             Bureau of Land Management
             San Juan Resource Area
             701 Camino del Rio
             Durango, CO 81301
             (303) 247-4082

CHIMNEY ROCK
ARCHAEOLOGICAL AREA

After you have visited a few Anasazi sites, you may begin to think that they chose the locations of their homes for the views. Chimney Rock will only reinforce that notion. The view is, in a word, stunning. But this may be too unscientific an explanation. Surely there must have been some unusual reason, for this high mountain location is uncharacteristic of the mesa and canyon-dwelling Anasazi.

Winter temperatures here along the Continental Divide often dip to thirty degrees below zero, and for several weeks each year daytime temperatures may only reach the teens. Despite these harsh conditions, the Anasazi lived here year-round—at 7,600 feet elevation—for two centu-

ries, from A.D. 900 until 1125. They built semisubterranean houses on knife-edge ridges, along with storage rooms and great kivas. To obtain water, they had to walk down to the Piedra River and Stollsteimer Creek and trudge back up the steep hill with heavy jugs.

The large pueblo at the top of the hill is of fine Chaco-style masonry architecture—a veneer of carefully worked and laid sandstone covering a rubble core. Chaco Canyon, ninety miles to the south, may be the clue to the Anasazi's presence at Chimney Rock. As Chaco Canyon ran out of wood, the people there may have turned to forested places like Chimney Rock to supply timbers. How they got the wood to Chaco remains a question—studies are being conducted that may provide some answers. At least 300 miles of roads radiated out from Chaco Canyon, and archeologists are looking for a road leading to Chimney Rock, believed to be the farthest northeast Chacoan outlier.

The moon may offer another explanation for the Chimney Rock site location. Astronomers have discovered that the full moon rises between the twin rock pinnacles during what is called a lunar standstill. The entire lunar standstill cycle—from the time of smallest angle of declination, to largest, and back to smallest—is 18.6 years. At its greatest declination, the moon appears to stand still, as the sun does during the solstices.

The first portion of the large Chaco-style pueblo at Chimney Rock was built in A.D. 1075, a year when the moon "stood still." An addition to the pueblo, clearly seen by the line where another rock wall abuts the main section, was added eighteen years later, in A.D. 1092.

The pinnacles themselves have been home to endangered peregrine falcons. A historic peregrine eyrie, or nesting site, is known to exist on one of the rock spires. Efforts to raise fledglings and have them return to the nest site have so far been unsuccessful. Nevertheless, a half-mile radius around the pinnacles is off-limits to visitors from March 1 through September 30 to protect the birds' potential habitat.

The 3,160-acre Chimney Rock Archaeological Area was established in 1970 under the jurisdiction of the San Juan National Forest. It is proposed for addition to the Chaco Archaeological Protection Site System.

LOCATION: 45 miles east of Durango on Highway 160; 17 miles west of Pagosa Springs. ACCESS: Turn south on Highway 151 at Arboles, Lake Capote, and Navajo Lake sign; go three miles to locked gate at Chimney Rock Area; entrance only on guided tour with a San Juan National Forest Association guide; drive another two miles up dirt road, park and walk the final one-half mile trail to the top. Tours are given four times daily, seven days per week, from May through September. Group size is limited to 30 people. For groups of 10 or more, call for reservations. FEE: Yes

CONTACT: San Juan National Forest
            Pagosa Ranger District
            Post Office Box 310
            Pagosa Springs, CO 81147
            (303) 264-2268

A good source for information on other Chacoan outliers in the Four Corners is a small book entitled *Chacoesque: Chaco-like Great Pueblo Architecture Outside Chaco Canyon*, written by Richard Flint and Shirley Flint, Villanueva, NM, 87583. It can be purchased at several bookstores in the region.

Square Tower Ruin, Mesa Verde National Park

Cliff Palace, Mesa Verde National Park

Escalante Ruin above Anasazi Heritage Center

Hovenweep Castle, Hovenweep National Monument, Sleeping Ute Mountain in the distance

Moonrise over Hovenweep Castle, Hovenweep National Monument

Cahone Group, Hovenweep National Monument

Horse Collar Ruins, Natural Bridges National Monument

Sipapu Bridge, Natural Bridges National Monument

Mountain sheep effigy (hollow) found in the Chimney Rock area

NORTHERN SAN JUAN

MESA VERDE NATIONAL PARK

What a striking view these ruins present at a distance! The explorer pictures to himself a whole town in miniature under the vault of rock in the cliff before him. But the town is a deserted one: not a sound breaks the silence, and not a movement meets the eye, among those gloomy, half-ruined walls, whose contours stand off sharply from the darkness of the inner cave.

—Gustaf Nordenskiöld

Cliff Palace

A young Swede and son of an arctic explorer, Gustaf Nordenskiöld found his way to the Southwest in 1891. A botanist in Denver had told him of the ruins on a high green plateau called Mesa Verde, and Nordenskiöld immediately contacted the men who could show him where

Mesa Verde's treasures were buried. Brothers Richard and Al Wetherill, Quakers who lived on their Alamo Ranch near the foot of the Mesa Verde, so kindled Gustaf's enthusiasm that he extended his week-long stay into several months that summer and fall.

Nordenskiöld photographed and excavated throughout the area, and in 1893 published a landmark report, *The Cliff Dwellers of the Mesa Verde*. He is credited with being the first person to describe scientifically those "gloomy" miniature towns he saw under the vaulted sandstone cliffs.

A hundred years after Nordenskiöld's first visit to the area, some of Mesa Verde's most precious artifacts found their way home. They had reposed in northern Europe all that time, shipped there by Nordenskiöld, and housed in Finland's National Museum in Helsinki. In the spring of

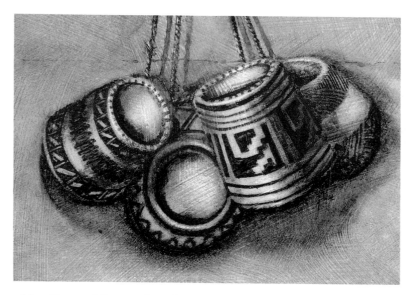

Mug House got its name from the mugs found hanging at the site

1991 the National Park Service was loaned many of those artifacts for an exhibit marking the centennial of Nordenskiöld's investigations in Mesa Verde.

Such special exhibits, as well as the permanent ones in the Chapin Mesa Museum, are excellent places to begin to learn about the riches of Mesa Verde. This park is by all measures the nation's gemstone of archeology. Each year nearly three-quarters of a million people drive up the winding road from the valley to visit the famous cliff dwellings. Among the most famous of the famous is Cliff Palace. Others are Spruce Tree House, Balcony House, Step House, Long House, Mug House and Far View House.

Visitors at Cliff Palace

Extensive archeological investigations since Nordenskiöld's time have revealed a great deal about the lives of the Anasazi in this stunning environment. Mesa Verde is the only place in the world where the entire sequence from Modified Basketmaker to middle Pueblo times, some 700 years, can be seen.

The Anasazi first settled in pithouses on the mesa top by A.D. 600, feeding themselves by farming, hunting, and gathering. A village of this era often included six to ten pithouses. Grandparents, parents, and children likely lived together in one of these small homes.

Around A.D. 750 the Anasazi started to build above-ground pueblos of worked sandstone blocks mortared with mud. A pueblo commonly arced around one of the pithouses which was eventually converted into a place where sacred ceremonies were held.

The number of inhabitants increased greatly, until nearly 2,500 lived on the mesa. But Mesa Verde was not the center that it appears to be; perhaps ten times this number of people were living in Montezuma Valley between present-day Cortez and Dove Creek, in very large settlements at places such as Lowry, Yellowjacket, Yucca House, and Goodman Point. From the Montezuma Valley Overlook along the main park road you can see what prehistoric Mesa Verdeans saw of their neighbors.

The well-known cliff dwellings of Mesa Verde were built at a late stage in Anasazi development, mostly in the mid-1200s. The Anasazi abandoned these dwellings—in fact the entire region—by A.D. 1300. Though they are still not sure, archeologists speculate that a combination of environmental and social causes were to blame for the abandonment. The spectacular cliff dwellings became the silent, deserted towns that Gustaf Nordenskiöld would write about in the nineteenth century.

On your visit to Mesa Verde, start at the Far View Visitor Center or Chapin Mesa Museum to obtain the latest schedules for visiting ruins and other places and events of interest in the park. An initial stop at Far View will save you a long drive, should any of the tours be canceled due to weather conditions.

Along the two, six-mile loop drives of the Ruins Road on Chapin Mesa, the following sites can be entered or viewed:

Spruce Tree House: 1/2-mile roundtrip, self-guided walk from Chapin Mesa Museum. Hiking in Mesa Verde is limited to established trails, two of which branch off the main Spruce Tree House trail: the 2.8-mile Petroglyph Point Trail climbs to the rim, while the 2.1-mile Spruce Canyon Trail stays in the canyon. Hikers must register with park rangers before leaving.

Cliff Palace: the largest cliff dwelling in North America, self-guided, 1/4-mile round-trip walk requires climbing four ladders into some of the 217 rooms and 23 kivas.

Balcony House: a medium-sized cliff dwelling of nearly forty rooms, with unique parapet walls and courtyard balcony. Entry only on ranger-led tour. Groups of up to fifty people leave from the parking lot at the overlook every half hour in summer. The free tours require climbing ladders and steps and crawling through a tunnel.

Square Tower House: a striking eighty-room cliff dwelling accessible by a 500-foot-long trail. Remains of sixty rooms and seven kivas can be seen now.

Some fifty additional cliff sites can be spotted from the Ruins Road.

A separate twelve-mile road curves up to *Wetherill Mesa*, on the western edge of Mesa Verde. This less-visited area of the park is accessible only in summer. An extensive archeological project on Wetherill Mesa in 1958 recorded 900 sites, from pithouses to cliff dwellings. Long House, the second largest cliff dwelling in the park, along with Step House, can be entered. Badger House Community, a complex on top of the mesa, can also be seen along a 3/4-mile trail.

LOCATION: 10 miles from Cortez, CO, and 36 miles from Durango on Highway 160. ACCESS: 21 miles on paved, winding road from main park entrance to Chapin Mesa and park headquarters. FEE: Yes.

CONTACT: Superintendent
             Mesa Verde National Park, CO 81330
             (505) 529-4461 or 529-4475

Balcony House

HOVENWEEP
NATIONAL MONUMENT

Boulder House and Holly House

Getting to this little-known and little-visited park strad-dling the border of southwest Colorado and southeast Utah is half the fun and what awaits you at Hovenweep National Monument is well worth the jostling ride over washboard roads. Past the Aneth oil fields where brawny pumps coax the Four Corners crude from the rock, through acres of gray-green sagebrush, you arrive at Hovenweep suddenly. At the end of the road sits a small and inviting visitor center with exhibits and book sales area, water cooler and coffee pot, and a reading area.

The visitor comment book contains proof that people who have made the effort to get here like their national parks this way—simple, peaceful, undeveloped. Even the rattlesnakes stay around. Warnings at trailheads about occasional snake sightings make you think twice about where you put your hands and feet.

Six major groups of ruins, in unconnected sections of the monument, are found up McElmo Creek and tributaries of Hovenweep Canyon, Bridge Canyon, and Ruin Canyon, all draining into the San Juan River. Of the six—Cajon, Holly, Hack-berry Canyon, Cutthroat Castle, Goodman Point, and Square Tower ruins— the Square Tower group just outside the visitor center is the most acces-sible.

Boulder House

From the visitor center a 0.3-mile trail leads to the foot of Hovenweep Castle. This trail, with self-guiding booklet, connects with two others—the mile-long Twin Towers and half-mile Tower Point loops. Winding between large boulders and over slickrock, the routes are marked generously with rock cairns. A little common sense and foresight will prevent getting seriously lost. Otherwise, Hovenweep is a place where you can wander a bit, with minimal development or restrictions beyond the necessary admonitions: don't stand or sit on the walls of the ruins and don't walk on the delicate microbiotic crust that protects the soil.

Hovenweep Castle, the stunning side-by-side pair known as Twin Towers, and others in the monument are awesome pieces of architecture. They seem to grow organically from the sandstone bedrock, their walls constructed of carefully dressed blocks, sometimes two or three courses thick and finished with mud plaster, and corners well made.

Though Hovenweep also contains pueblos and cliff dwellings, towers are justifiably its claim to fame. And Hovenweep is not an isolated instance. Hundreds of such towers exist in the area—one, two, and three stories high—beside springs in the heads of canyons and standing on mesa tops. Some are circular, others square, still others D-shaped. The uses of the towers are uncertain. They may have been fortifications, a move the Anasazi may have found necessary to protect themselves against the scourge of juniper midges, or biting gnats, that thrive at this elevation from mid-May through July. Or perhaps they were huge storage silos (cultivated crops were found in every canyon-head tower visited by archeologist Joseph Winter). They may have been ceremonial places (in some earlier towers on the mesa top, tunnels lead to nearby kivas). Alternatively, they may have served as astronomical observatories. Though windows or doors are uncommon, many of the towers do have portholes in the walls through which beams of sunlight shine on summer and winter solstices.

Though the Anasazi lived on Cajon Mesa until 1300, after 1150 many left their mesa-top villages and moved to the canyon heads where they built the enigmatic towers. The towers were built between A.D. 1163 and 1277, though most after 1230. The canyon heads were advantageous because the farmers could practice water control, catching and channeling rainfall coming off the rims. And they are the places where most plants and small animals are found.

William Henry Jackson, photographing and surveying for the U.S. Geological Survey in southwest Colorado in 1874, was the first to use Ute word "hovenweep," which

Cajon Group

means deserted valley. Though it had been deserted for nearly five centuries when Jackson saw it, Hovenweep formerly had been home to people for thousands of years. Hunters camped around Cajon Springs on the southern end of Cajon Mesa as long as 14,000 years ago. Though Anasazi farmers had settled in the Four Corners by A.D. 1, they didn't move into Hovenweep until after A.D. 500. After A.D. 750 the number of hamlets tripled; population continued to increase after A.D. 900, and Hovenweep marked the northern frontier of the Anasazi. The Anasazi were probably farming the mesa tops, building checkdams to collect soil and water for their gardens. A reconstructed example of such a checkdam can be seen along the Square Tower Loop trail.

LOCATION: 45 miles west of Cortez, CO; 45 miles east of Blanding, UT. ACCESS: Dirt roads negotiable by normal passenger vehicles enter from several directions; follow signs to Hovenweep. From Cortez up McElmo Canyon the road is rough but passable year-round; road in from Pleasant View (past Cutthroat Castle, part of Hovenweep NM, and access to Painted Hand Pueblo) summer only. FEE: None.

CONTACT: Superintendent
             Hovenweep National Monument
             McElmo Route
             Cortez, CO 81321
             (303) 529-4465

NATURAL BRIDGES
NATIONAL MONUMENT

HORSE COLLAR RUIN

This small cliff dwelling is actually two groups of ruins tucked under a pair of alcoves in White Canyon. The name "Horse Collar" comes from the molded adobe doorways on the pair of storage rooms at the site that reminded someone of leather horse collars.

In 1937 National Park Service archeologist Charlie Steen investigated this site and found the two storage rooms, five houses, and two kivas under the southern alcove well preserved. Steen planned to work on the roofed kiva, but was so excited by the round storage rooms that he also decided to "clean out" one of them to "arrange for their preservation."

What interested Steen about the storage room was the wall construction and doorway shape. The walls were built of sandstone slabs and river cobbles, held in place by adobe. Around the outside of the small heart-shaped doorways (by Steen's description) was a pronounced mud molding. Inside the room he noted four plugs of wood embedded in the walls about three feet above the floor, spaced at equal quarters around the walls. On the floor he found burned roof debris, mostly adobe, and wands of willow.

The kiva too was a marvel of preservation when Steen found it. He remarked that, "A fine looking, rectangular roofed kiva with original ladder poles protruding through the hatch is not found every day." A plastered adobe ramp nearly fifteen feet long led from the floor of the rock shelter to the hatch of the kiva. Steen could readily discern that its roof was made of large cottonwood vigas, juniper poles and shakes, and mud.

Horse Collar Ruin

Kivas of this area are distinct. There are many of them, and sometimes they occur either alone or with storage structures, as at Horse Collar. Though most kivas were used for ceremony, in this region they seem to have been used mainly as dwellings.

Horse Collar may have been inhabited as early as Basketmaker times, but tree-ring dates on wood from the kiva (ca A.D. 1208) indicate it was also one of the latest Pueblo sites occupied in Natural Bridges. The Anasazi were gone from Natural Bridges by 1250, from almost all the Four Corners region about forty years later.

The Natural Bridges-White Canyon area is on the northern boundary between Anasazi and Fremont, the contemporaneous culture that lived throughout Utah. Prehistoric sites in the area are especially interesting because they show "hybrid" features of both cultures, an indication of their intermingling here.

LOCATION: 40 miles west of Blanding, UT on Utah 95. ACCESS: A 0.3-mile trail along the 9-mile paved Bridge View Drive in park leads to ruin overlook. Ruin is located above creekbed in two alcoves on far wall of White Canyon. Check at visitor center for directions to hike to ruin itself. FEE: Yes, entrance fee to park in summer.

CONTACT: Superintendent
           Box 1 Natural Bridges
           Lake Powell, UT 84533
           (802) 259-5174

CANYONLANDS AND ARCHES NATIONAL PARKS

Canyonlands and Arches, like Natural Bridges, are at a cultural borderland between the Four Corners Anasazi and the Fremont, who lived farther north in Utah. The meeting of the two cultures here left a mixed signature.

Landscape Arch

The wilderness wonderlands of Canyonlands and Arches are rich in archeology, though most is of the backcountry genre. Indeed, an intrepid explorer could spend a lifetime jeeping, hiking, or mountain biking the trails and back roads of these parks.

One site in the Needles District of Canyonlands, however, is easily accessible in any type of vehicle. *Roadside Ruin* is a granary reached along a third-mile loop trail near the Needles Visitor Center. Hidden by juniper trees and well protected under a rock alcove, the granary is excellently preserved. It is typical of sites found in Canyonlands, an area used during prehistoric times more for storage than for living, possibly because the land here receives so little rainfall.

Around A.D. 950 an overflow of people from the Mesa Verde area did begin to settle in Canyonlands. They grew the traditional crops here, but also knew how to exploit native plants such as Indian ricegrass, Fremont barberry, and four-wing saltbush. They stored the surplus in granaries like the one at Roadside Ruin.

All other sites in the Needles District require four-wheel-drive, and in most cases a hike, to reach. The Salt Creek area has been designated an archaeological district for its concentration of Pueblo period sites. The *Peek-a-Boo rock art panel* is one such site, accessible from the Peek-a-Boo campsite four miles in on the Salt Creek Road. The road is marked, but requires a vehicle that can negotiate deep sand and fairly high water at certain times of year. A small sign announces the site, which shows an early rock art style called Barrier Canyon, with  shield figures, dots, and other Anasazi trademarks super-imposed.

Also located in the Salt Creek district is the largest masonry structure in the park, called *Big Ruin*. Another late Anasazi site is *Tower Ruin*, five miles in on the Salt Creek Road, perched high on the walls of a redrock canyon.

Canyonlands is famous for one place in particular— *Barrier* (or Horseshoe) *Canyon*. This small, unconnected parcel of land is located west of the main park area in the

Maze District. Some of the best-known rock art sites in the canyon are the Horseshoe Shelter, Great Gallery, and High Gallery. The human-shaped figures on these panels are huge and haunting. Those in the Great Gallery, painted on the wall in red and white, are nearly life-size, staring out with ghostly eyes.

"The Ghost" at Horseshoe (Barrier) Canyon

Barrier Canyon is the "type section" for this style of rock art, which is dated between 500 B.C. to A.D. 500. The Barrier Canyon style thus is older than and different from that of Anasazi or Fremont. It is a world-class style, known over a wide area from as far as Grand Canyon in northern

Arizona to the White River in northwest Colorado. Park rangers sometimes lead hikes into Barrier Canyon as staff is available. Contact the Hans Flat Ranger Station, (801) 259-6513, for current information.

Interesting rock art may also be seen in Arches National Park. One of the most popular examples adorns a cliff at the mouth of *Courthouse Wash*. Park at the pull-out along Utah 191, two miles north of Moab on the right (east) side of the highway. A short trail up the hill behind you leads to this striking panel which displays an unusual collection of several styles: Barrier Canyon, late

Courthouse Towers

Anasazi, Fremont, and historic Ute or Navajo elements. *Wolfe Ranch*, near Delicate Arch, is best known for the historic buildings there. But Ute Indians also knew the place, and drew pictographs of a horse, bighorn sheep, and figures on horseback.

CONTACT: Superintendent
             Canyonlands National Park
             125 West 200 South
             Moab, UT 84532
             (801) 259-7164

NEWSPAPER ROCK STATE PARK

Indian Creek has always attracted people. A year-round source of water and a natural passageway, it has for thousands of years invited people to linger. And as they paused there, they practiced their artistry on the burnished rock faces, leaving one of the finest and most accessible rock art displays in the Southwest.

Hundreds of figures and symbols have been etched on a single, gigantic sandstone boulder where Indian Creek canyon narrows. All are petroglyphs, chipped into the desert varnish rather than painted on, revealing the creamy natural color of the sandstone. The art at Newspaper Rock is outstanding for the span of time represented. Some specimens date from the Archaic period, more than 1,500 years ago, others are less than 200 years old. A study of the montage of squiggles, animals, and footprints reveals that most are Anasazi style, though prehistoric Fremont who lived to the north and historic Ute and Navajo figures are also represented. One Ute image is of a person on horseback, shooting an arrow at a game animal.

Indian Creek invites us to slow down and look for the many other displays of rock art that line its course, including ones at Shay Canyon about two miles west of Newspaper Rock.

Mastadon Rock, Shay Canyon

LOCATION: 13 miles north of Monticello, about 40 miles south of Moab. ACCESS: Highway 211 (road into Needles District of Canyonlands), within 60 yards of highway on north side. FEE: No

CONTACT: Bureau of Land Management
             P.O. Box 7
             435 N. Main
             Monticello, UT 84535
             (801) 587-2141

Beef Basin/Ruin Park

An extremely remote, world-class archaeological site, Beef Basin/Ruin Park, is also accessible off Highway 211 into the Needles District. Among the piñon-juniper forest of Beef Basin rise several of the enigmatic stone towers built during the thirteenth century. The towers sit at the edge of the more open Ruin Park area. This is difficult country to get into; before embarking on a journey into Beef Basin/Ruin Park, contact the Bureau of Land Management office in Monticello, Utah, at (801) 587-2141.

GRAND GULCH PRIMITIVE AREA
CEDAR MESA

Spectacular Grand Gulch heads in piñon-juniper country at 6,800 feet on Grand Gulch Plateau north of Natural Bridges. Draining the west side of Cedar Mesa, the canyon drops 3,000 feet on its twisting fifty-mile course to the San Juan River.

The gulch was named by Mormon pioneers who encountered it during a mission to settle Bluff, Utah, in the winter of 1880. Wagons, mules, and people had just accomplished a harrowing descent through Hole-in-the-Rock to cross the Colorado River. As the hardy pioneers traveled east, the impassable walls of Cedar Mesa Sandstone that make up most of Grand Gulch forced them to the head of the canyon and earned the gulch its name.

Charles McLoyd and C. Graham of Durango, Colorado, began excavating archaeological sites in Grand Gulch in 1890. The artifacts they collected went to the University of Pennsylvania Museum and the American Museum of Natural History. Famous Mesa Verde pioneer Richard Wetherill came to Grand Gulch shortly thereafter, leading the Hyde Exploring Expedition of the American Museum of Natural History from 1893 to 1897.

From finds in Grand Gulch, Wetherill astutely observed that predecessors of the cliff dwellers had lived here. For the incredible woven materials found in Grand Gulch (and

One variation of spaced coil technique -- coils held apart by false knots

Coiled center of basket -- technique used Basket Maker II to Modern

One variation of close coil technique -- coils drawn snugly together

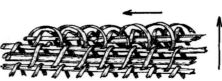

Tapered twill rim -- technique used Basket Maker II to Modern

Butler Wash), Wetherill coined the term "Basket People" to apply to these Anasazi who lived here as early as A.D. 200. Wetherill's category has stood through nearly a century of additional archaeological work.

Grand Gulch, and Cedar Mesa, constitute one of the world's premier backcountry archaeology areas, with literally thousands of intact cliff dwellings and rock art panels. Dayhiking is possible, but backpacking in for several days is the only way to really begin to appreciate this 400,000-acre wilderness.

Water is scarce most of the time, except in late summer, when the steep canyons are prone to flashflood during heavy storms. Summers are blazing and winters are frigid. Scorpions, rattlesnakes, and a number of other desert dwellers now inhabit Grand Gulch. Be prepared. Get maps, find out about water sources, and register at the Kane Gulch Ranger Station before embarking on a hike into this remote area.

LOCATION: Off Utah 261, approximately 25 miles west of Blanding and 10 miles north of Mexican Hat, Utah. ACCESS: Major trailheads on east side are Kane Gulch and Bullet Canyon; from west, Collins Spring trailhead off Utah 276. FEE: Yes

CONTACT: Bureau of Land Management
             Box 7, 435 Main Street
             Monticello, UT 84535
             (801) 587-2141

OR: Kane Gulch Ranger Station (main trailhead)
             on UT 261, 4 mi. south of UT 95

TRAIL OF THE ANCIENTS
BLANDING TO NATURAL BRIDGES

Backcountry kiva

Utah's scenic Bicentennial Highway 95 follows the path of what at least one local group has dubbed, with good reason, The Trail of the Ancients. This road, from Blanding past Natural Bridges, offers access to a number of ruins, most managed by the federal Bureau of Land Management.

Thirty miles west of Blanding is *Mule Canyon*, just off Highway 95 on the north. A paved, wheelchair-accessible trail winds through the site, which includes an L-shaped, twelve-room pueblo, a kiva, and the remnants of a tower. All of these are connected by tunnels built by the prehistoric inhabitants as quick—and perhaps secret—passageways. The kiva has been covered with a roof to protect it from the elements. The kiva's round shape is characteristic of the Northern San Juan/Mesa Verde people, though there is also sign of Kayenta activity at Mule Canyon.

The Anasazi lived here primarily from A.D. 1000 to 1150, though the site was occupied as early at A.D. 750. Mule Canyon is a fine rest stop and a good place to enjoy a picnic lunch.

The tower at Mule Canyon is within view of another site about a mile to the southeast known as *Cave Towers*. This group of stone towers, arranged in a semicircle, is situated at the head of Mule Canyon. Possibly the towers were located here to protect one of the most precious treasures of the Anasazi, a permanent spring.

Some have theorized that such towers, found through-out this part of the Four Corners, served as a communications system. Their location appears to have been planned, so that signals, perhaps sent by fires, could be flashed from one village to another. The half-mile road to Cave Towers, a fragile site, is unmarked and very rough.

At *Arch Canyon* a perennial stream flows beneath the shade of green cottonwoods, and great arches of sandstone rise in the upper reaches of the canyon. Storage rooms called granaries, believed to date to A.D. 1050 and 1150, dot the walls of the canyon. A few Anasazi dwellings can be found on the mesa top.

Arch Canyon is accessible on a two-mile dirt road running north off Utah 95. Heading west out of Blanding, follow Highway 95 for seventeen miles. Turn north (right) between mileposts 107 and 108 . About two miles up the road is a parking area. From there a quarter-mile trail leads to the overlook. Binoculars are helpful to spot the sites.

A lovely site within easy walking distance of Utah 95 is *Butler Wash Ruins and Overlook*, thirteen miles west of

Blanding. The overlook lies at the end of a one-mile self-guiding loop trail. From the parking area, follow rock cairns which mark the trail. As you stroll along the sandstone caprock with the brochure in hand, you can learn a little botany and geology. If it is late August, and still very warm in midday, the prickly pear cactus along the trail will be sporting lush red fruits.

At the end of the trail, the Butler Wash overlook affords a closeup view of the ruins, perched in cool alcoves at the head of the wash. Here the Anasazi built homes about 700 years ago and held ceremonies in the four kivas. Three are round—Mesa Verde style—while one is square—Kayenta style. The large streamed of Butler Wash, which eventually drains into the San Juan River, provided the Anasazi with plentiful farmland.

Butler Wash Ruins

BLANDING - BLUFF AREA

Several backcountry sites can be found on Bureau of Land Management lands east of Blanding and near Bluff, Utah. *Three Kiva Pueblo* was named for a trio of round kivas in the center of this village. One has been fully restored and can be entered. Inside are the classic features that say "kiva"—a bench encircling the room, stone pilasters that supported the roof beams, a firepit with a deflector, and a ventilator shaft that let out smoky air and permitted fresh air to enter. One other feature, the hole in the center of the floor called the *sipapu*, is the symbolic place where the people emerged from the underworld.

In addition to the kiva, fourteen rooms have been excavated at Three Kiva. Archeologists also found a ramada area and a long narrow structure they call the "turkey pen" because it contained many bones of turkeys, believed to have been raised for their feathers. The Three Kiva site was occupied for three centuries, between A.D. 1000 and 1300.

To reach Three Kiva travel two miles south of Blanding on Highway 191, turn east (left) onto a gravel county road, C-219, then follow C-206 for twenty miles. Turn north on C-146, a graded dirt road for seven more miles to Three Kiva.

Alkali Ridge was excavated by Harvard archeologist J.O. Brew in the 1930s. The site is significant as the place where the earliest Pueblo period, Pueblo I, was defined. The site, now a National Historic Landmark, is located on a county road six miles east of Blanding, off Highway 191.

A very accessible rock art panel, nearly a mile long, can be seen at *Sand Island Recreation Site,* two miles west of Bluff. On a cliff near the boat launch for the San Juan River are some spectacular petroglyphs, including striking examples of the figure called Kokopelli. Commonly known as the humpbacked flute player, Kokopelli is also widely known for his outstanding male appendage, often graphically depicted in Anasazi rock art.

Six miles by boat downriver from Sand Island is the beautiful ruin called *River House*. Built in an alcove on the north side of the San Juan, River House was occupied between A.D. 900 and 1300. A captivating snake pictograph adorns the alcove wall above the pueblo's fourteen rooms. The corncobs still found in River House are evidence of

A section of River House

the occupation of its inhabitants. Both Mesa Verde and Kayenta style pottery have been identified in the ruins, though the masonry style is predominantly Kayenta.

San Juan Anthropomorphs at Butler Wash

CONTACT: Bureau of Land Management
San Juan Resource Area
P.O. Box 7, 435 N. Main Street
Monticello, UT 84535
(801) 587-2141

KAYENTA

White House Ruin, Canyon De Chelly

CANYON DE CHELLY
NATIONAL MONUMENT

Strong winds blow on a summer evening at Canyon de Chelly, sending cottonwood fluff flying through the air. Soft voices speaking Navajo are heard everywhere. The magic of this place is sensed immediately upon entering. Here people of several cultures have lived for 1,500 years.

The tapestried stone walls, soaring alcoves, and sandy streambeds are filled with the homes not only of modern-day Navajo Indians, but also those who came earlier: the Anasazi. Nearly 800 prehistoric and historic sites are known within the monument's 131 square miles.

To really begin to appreciate this place, leave behind the air-conditioned comfort of the family van and go afoot. That is how the Anasazi went everywhere. By traveling this way, albeit in tennis shoes rather than yucca sandals, we can still feel the gritty sand grains, smell the strong scent of juniper trees, see the orange cliffs pressed against turquoise sky, and hear the silence of the canyons. This is the way to know the invigoration of cool shade and the debilitation of full sun. We can appreciate too the happiness of rounding a bend and seeing your home—for an Anasazi a mud and plaster cliff dwelling under a sheltering alcove; for a Navajo, the many-sided log hogan and sheep corral.

One of the best ways to experience these things is to walk the one-and-a-quarter-mile trail down to *White House Ruin*. This is the only ruin in the park accessible without a Navajo or Park Service guide. Though Canyon de Chelly is designated a national monument, it lies entirely on the Navajo Indian Reservation, and all visitors are guests of the Navajo people.

From the roadside overlook, the white plastered walls of upper White House Ruin gleam against the tawny sandstone. About 150 yards to the right of the overlook, the trail descends. Down the slope, through piñon and juniper and cactus, you suddenly find yourself *within* the canyon. Just at the bottom of the trail you will get a close view of a traditional Navajo hogan, with prickly pear cacti growing from the mud roof.

White House Ruin

Once in the streambed, you will feel the effort of walking through soft sand. In spring the wash is usually flowing, and quicksand may be a problem. In the absence of runoff, the stream is only a trickle and forms no obstacle. White House Ruin is hidden behind a line of cottonwoods, and reveals itself only after you are on the far side of the creek. In summer, even in early morning, the shade of the cottonwoods is welcome.

Lieutenant James Simpson, detailed to explore the Southwest in 1848, named the ruin Casa Blanca—White House—for the striking color of the plaster applied by Anasazi hands nearly six hundred years earlier. To the Navajo it is *Kinii Na'igai*, "White House In Between." We now view it through wire fencing, for the ruin is closed to entry to protect its crumbling walls from the footsteps of the thousands who come each year. A stone wall and reinforced streambanks were built by the Park Service to protect the ruin from the floodwaters of Rio de Chelly.

The upper and lower portions of White House Ruin may have contained up to eighty rooms at one time. Because of stream erosion, only about sixty rooms remain. Rooms of the lower ruin once may have reached to within four feet of the upper ruin. Four round ceremonial structures, called kivas, have also been counted here. One in the lower ruin bears many layers of plaster, a chore undertaken periodically perhaps by keepers of the kivas. Dates from the rings of trees used in White House show that construction first took place about A.D. 1060 and lasted until A.D. 1275.

Even the earliest Anasazi chose alcoves such as this in which to build their homes. A pithouse in Mummy Cave in Canyon del Muerto has been dated to A.D. 306, Basket-maker times. The perishable items they made, such as split yucca baskets and fur blankets, have been well preserved in the caves and alcoves. Early Basketmakers also grew corn and squash and hunted deer and rabbits in the area, and began to make pottery around A.D. 500.

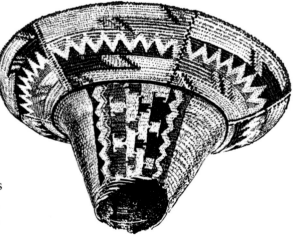

Black and red Basketmaker II carrying basket

This stage was also marked by the addition of cotton and beans to their crop repertoire. As the population began to grow, they continued to live in the circular, semisubterranean houses under the alcoves, where families huddled around the firepit of their pithouse as snow dusted the cliffs during a winter storm.

Around A.D. 850 the Anasazi in Canyon de Chelly adopted pueblo architecture, building above-ground masonry rooms in villages. Antelope House, Big Cave, and Mummy Cave are among these sites, where extended families began to live together in larger groups. Their masonry was cruder than that of the Mesa Verdeans and Chacoans, and their pottery was of the same type as that found throughout the Kayenta area—corrugated and black-and-white wares with characteristic geometric designs.

Farming was their mainstay, and they used both the tops of the plateau and the canyon bottoms where water and flat land were available. Between A.D. 1050 and 1150, years of good rainfall, agriculture was at its most productive in Canyon de Chelly. This was also a time of dramatic population increase.

After 1150, a period of less precipitation may have turned the people's focus entirely to the canyons, where water might be more readily available. Villages were fewer, but larger and better built. Antelope House, White House, Mummy Cave, and Sliding Rock were among the villages of this period, and various ones show masonry typical of both Chaco Canyon and Mesa Verde. Refugees from these areas possibly were entering Canyon de Chelly at this time, and at some sites such as Antelope House, two different social groups (apparently) live amicably in the same place, separated by nothing more than a central plaza.

Despite this supposed influx of outsiders, population in the Canyon de Chelly area declined after A.D. 1150. The cliff dwellings were abandoned by A.D. 1300. An eroding streambed may have caused the residents of Antelope House to vacate. Today, as you view Antelope House from the overlook, the sand-filled rooms still provide stark evidence for this. Washed out fields and lack of firewood and timber may have led to the departure of other residents.

But the old houses were not abandoned forever. Hopi Indians came from the south and added on to some of them. The peach trees found in Canyon de Chelly, introduced by the Spaniards, may have been planted and harvested by the Hopi. Around 1750, Canyon de Chelly saw the arrival of the *Dinè*, the Navajos. These Athapaskan speakers, who had entered the Southwest possibly by the 1500s, were hunters, farmers and herders. They built their round hogans and planted crops in the canyons in the summer, coming out to the warmer plateaus in winter. Today you can still see their homes and fields, and hear the sound of sheep bells in the canyon bottoms.

As the pueblo dwellers had before them, Navajos found the fastnesses of Canyon de Chelly a refuge—first from Spaniards and then from soldiers of the United States Army—both trying to oust them from their lands. The names Antonio Narbona (a Spanish lieutenant) and Albert Pfeiffer (a U.S. Army captain) are infamous among the Navajos. On a frozen January day in 1864 Captain Pfeiffer swept down Canyon del Muerto, taking Navajo prisoners. Many hid among the crevices of an inaccessible rock butte called Navajo Fortress, that can be seen from the Antelope House Overlook.

After this raid, 500 Navajos finally surrendered, ending a long era of pursuit. Three months later the dark "Long

Walk" began. Some 2,400 Navajos, most of them on foot, made the 300-mile journey to Bosque Redondo (Fort Sumner) in eastern New Mexico. Joined by thousands of others, they endured four years of near-famine existence, until a peace treaty granted them three and half million acres of land as a tribal reservation. Included was their old home and last stronghold, Canyon de Chelly.

Guide describing Navajo Fortress

Spider Rock

LOCATION: Off Highway 191, three miles from Chinle, Arizona.

ACCESS: Two paved roads: 36-mile South Rim Drive leading to Tsegi, Junction, White House, Sliding House, Face Rock, and Spider Rock overlooks; and North Rim Drive, 34-mile round trip, leading to Antelope House, Mummy Cave, and Massacre Cave overlooks. Road guides available at visitor center. With the exception of hike to White House Ruin, travel is allowed in the canyons ONLY with park ranger or authorized Navajo guide. FEE: None to enter monument or hike to White House Ruin. Fees are charged for guided jeep and horseback tours run by private concessionaires. Check at the visitor center for information.

CONTACT: Superintendent
Canyon de Chelly National Monument
P.O. Box 588
Chinle, AZ 86503
(602) 674-5436

NAVAJO NATIONAL MONUMENT

Betatakin

The Navajos call them *tse yaa kin*, "houses beneath the rock." But the magnificent cliff dwellings of Betatakin and Keet Seel in Navajo National Monument were not home to the ancestors of the Navajo. They were, instead, the homes of the pueblo-dwelling Anasazi during the A.D. 1200s. The Anasazi chose the convoluted canyons of the Tsegi system in which to farm and make their living, but only for a short time.

You can first glimpse *Betatakin* from the overlook at the

end of the half-mile Sandal Trail that leads from the visitor center. So well hidden is it under the sweep of the huge alcove that you may not at first notice the dwelling. Betatakin's 135 rooms, built of local sandstone, follow the curve of the cave wall, noticeable finally because of the silhouette openings of the small windows and doors. Scale is difficult to appreciate from this perspective. The cave itself is 370 feet wide and 450 feet high, and it is carved into a cliff 800 feet high.

A thick, and unusual, stand of aspen and water birch clogs the small tributary canyon in front of Betatakin. The cool air and water flowing off the slickrock walls and dripping from a small spring under the alcove let the trees live here. The water, the trees, and the protection of the cliff are undoubtedly what attracted the Anasazi. An advance group first occupied Betatakin by A.D. 1250. Other families followed some fifteen years later, perhaps from nearby Long House Valley, then gripped in drought. These pioneers apparently cut and stockpiled timber in anticipation of the arrival of still more people, who came in 1275.

The original timbers are still in place in the roofs of the well-preserved cliff dwelling. Though Anasazi farmers went to great lengths to build Betatakin, they stayed only about fifty years. Tree-ring dates indicate that the final occupation of Betatakin was in A.D. 1286. Perhaps the people were continuing to move farther up into the cliffs and canyon heads to stay ahead of eroding stream courses that would have destroyed their farmlands.

The only way to enter Betatakin is to hike the two and half miles into the canyon with a ranger. The trail descends nearly a thousand feet from the rim to the canyon, and it is a thousand foot climb back out. Register for these popular daily trips at the visitor center as soon as it opens the day you wish to go. Group size is limited to twenty-four, and the tours are conducted only in the summer months.

Keet Seel, Navajo for "broken pieces of pottery," is one of the most spectacular ruins in the Southwest. This 160-room cliff dwelling with a 180-foot masonry wall is the largest in

Keet Seel

Arizona. The Anasazi lived here much earlier than at Betatakin, as early as A.D. 950. The Anasazi who followed after this first group left reused the same rock and wood to build the final dwelling that we see today. Around A.D. 1272 a building boom occurred, and Keet Seel was expanded to house a growing population. The same environmental forces that led to Betatakin's abandonment around A.D. 1300 probably also caused people to leave Keet Seel for good.

To reach Keet Seel, you must walk or ride a horse eight

miles (one-way) up a colorful redrock canyon, often in the streambed. There is a primitive campground near the ruin for overnight hikers. Keet Seel is open only on selected days of the week during the summer, and you must be accompanied by a ranger to enter the ruins. Reservations can be made two months in advance, and group size is limited to twenty people. Once there, place your hand beside one of their handprints painted on the wall, and you will feel an unspoken but powerful human bond with these ancient people.

LOCATION: 20 miles west of Kayenta, Arizona, off Highway 160. ACCESS: Nine-mile paved road, AZ 564, off Highway 160, to visitor center and Betatakin. Keet Seel is a sixteen-mile roundtrip hike or horseback ride. Open from Memorial Day to Labor Day. Horseback trips are conducted by a private party and can be arranged through monument staff. FEE: None to monument or ruins; Yes, for horseback rides.

CONTACT: Superintendent
            Navajo National Monument
            HC71- Box 3
            Tonalea, AZ 86044
            (602) 672-2366

TUSAYAN AND WALHALLA GLADES, GRAND CANYON NATIONAL PARK

Kwagunt Canyon enters Grand Canyon at mile 56

Did prehistoric people, from the rooftops of their pueblos, savor Grand Canyon sunsets as we do today? We'll never know, and can only hope they did. What we do know, though, is that people have lived in and used the Grand Canyon for thousands of years. More than 2,800 archeological sites have been recorded in the park, testimony to the extent of its use.

Evidence of the earliest inhabitants was found one day in 1933 when young men of the Civilian Conservation Corps were exploring a cave on the north side of the canyon. In the cave in the Redwall Limestone they discovered some willow twig figures twisted into the shape of what looked like bighorn sheep.

Many split-twig figurines have since been found in other caves in the Grand Canyon, finely preserved in these dry, sheltered environments. Fearing the figurines might be removed by amateurs, archeologists carried them out of the canyon, and to laboratories where they have been studied and placed for safekeeping.

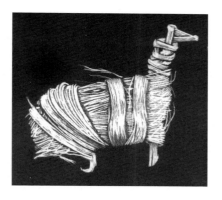

The twig figurines may have been left by hunters four thousand years ago. As they searched the canyon walls for elusive bighorn sheep, perhaps they offered them as charms to bring luck in their hunt.

People did live in the canyon in late Archaic and early Basketmaker times, but on a limited basis. Around A.D. 500, however, the Anasazi arrived, digging pithouse homes and weaving fine yucca baskets. By A.D. 1000 they were building pueblos, making pottery, and growing a good share of their food. The Anasazi heyday in the Grand Canyon was between the years A.D. 1050 and 1150.

One of the best examples of a pueblo of this time period is at *Tusayan* on the South Rim near Desert View. Here a very fine museum orients visitors to the site. The late Emil Haury, dean of Southwestern archeology, excavated Tusayan Pueblo in 1930. Tusayan is small—only about thirty people lived in its fifteen rooms. The Anasazi who settled here were associated with the Kayenta branch, and in the Grand Canyon were at the farthest western part of their territory. They stayed on the rim long enough to plant fields and build checkdams to capture water and soil; remnants of these can be seen along the path through the ruin. The pueblo was occupied until about A.D. 1225.

Another easily accessible ruin at Grand Canyon is on the North Rim. *Walhalla Glades,* near Cape Royal, was surveyed in the late 1930s by Edward T. Hall, Jr. Here at 8,000 feet above sea level the Anasazi made a sort of summer home, an escape from the searing temperatures of the inner canyon and a place where they could grow food.

Archeologists who have worked on Walhalla Glades and down Unkar Creek to Unkar Delta on the Colorado River, think the Anasazi moved up onto the plateau when the delta became overcrowded. Unkar Creek was their primary route to Walhalla Glades, a peninsula that juts out into the canyon from the Walhalla Plateau. The ever observant Anasazi realized that the peninsula was a good place to grow corn because it benefited from warm updrafts rising out of the canyon.

Sites where food was processed and stored have even been identified on two isolated buttes—Sky Island and Wotan's Throne—off Walhalla Plateau. Such sites hint that times may have gotten very difficult for the Anasazi as they tried to farm at this elevation. Marginal already, farming here came to an end during the drought years of the early twelfth century.

For about a hundred years, from A.D. 1050 to 1150, possibly twenty people lived at Walhalla Glades. The excavated portion of the site contains four large rooms and two unconnected smaller rooms, probably used for storage. Room walls were built of blocks of creamy Kaibab limestone. A great deal of rubble was found in the rooms from roofs that had burned and collapsed. At hearths in the centers of the floors, the Anasazi cooked their corn

Granaries at Nankoweep

meal mush and warmed their hands on chilly North Rim nights.

In the two small rooms, two adult males were found buried, each with offerings of pottery bowls. They were two of only four burials found on the entire Walhalla Plateau during excavations in the late 1960s.

LOCATION: *Tusayan Ruin*, 20 miles from Grand Canyon Village on East Rim Drive. ACCESS: 0.1-mile wheelchair-accessible paved trail, leads through ruin. FEE: Entrance fee to Grand Canyon National Park; none to ruin. Open year-round.

CONTACT: Tusayan Museum at (602) 638-7893

Walhalla Glades is 22 miles from Grand Canyon Lodge on the road to Cape Royal. ACCESS: Short trail to ruin from marked parking area along road. The North Rim is closed from mid-October to mid-May due to snow. FEE: Entrance fee to park, none to ruin.

CONTACT: North Rim Interpretation at (602) 638-7739, mid-May to mid-October.

Kiva, Grand Gulch Primitive Area

The singular "All American Man" three color shield figure pictograph, Canyonlands National Park

Pictographs and balcony, Grand Gulch Primitive Area

Delicate Arch frames the La Sal Mountains, Arches National Park

Cave Towers, Cedar Mesa

Wupatki Pueblo, Wupatki National Monument—900 years ago this area was blanketed with cinders from the eruption of Sunset Crater

Lomaki Ruin, Wupatki National Monument, San Francisco Peaks to the west

Comb Ridge and the Abajo Mountains

ON THE FRINGES
WUPATKI NATIONAL MONUMENT

Sunset Crater

At first sight, neighboring Wupatki and Sunset Crater in northern Arizona may seem distinctly unrelated. While Wupatki's redrock ruins rise above grassy valleys, the landscape of Sunset Crater is tortured black rock and stunted trees.

But in A.D. 1064 the people of Wupatki were keenly aware of the Sunset Crater region to the south. In this year the volcano that created the crater blew its top. The people likely had forewarning, for the ground probably trembled before the first violent eruption. With the explosion (and the many others that followed) came hot, noxious gases, raging fires, and molten lava that destroyed the people's fields and buried their homes.

The Indians of the Wupatki area fled their earthen lodges, but returned after things cooled. They began to build the beautiful multistory pueblos we see today preserved within Wupatki National Monument. The traditional explanation of this renaissance was propounded by Harold Colton, founder of the Museum of Northern Arizona in Flagstaff.

Colton named the culture of Wupatki the Sinagua, a Spanish word meaning "without water," for the waterless region they inhabited. Dr. Colton believed the Sinagua had farmed in the grassy parks around the San Francisco Peaks as early as A.D. 500 or 600. With the eruption of Sunset Crater, they received a blessing in disguise. The fine ash and cinders that covered the ground after the eruption actually created good mulch. When the Sinagua returned, they found new fertile ground for their fields.

Dr. Colton further believed the Sinagua were joined by the Kayenta Anasazi from the north, who either built, or taught the Sinagua how to build, the masonry pueblos. The Hohokam of the Salt-Gila river basins near present-day Phoenix also joined the land rush. They introduced the idea of ballcourts, one of which can be seen beside Wupatki Pueblo.

Evidence uncovered since Dr. Colton's work in the 1930s and 1940s has led to a revised view of the Wupatki/Sunset Crater Sinagua. Archeologist Peter

Ballcourt at Wupatki Pueblo

Pilles and others think that the beneficial effects of the cinder mulch have been overstated. And rather than a wholesale migration of different people into the area, he thinks the Sinagua themselves adopted the outsiders' architecture and pottery. The exotic jewelry, pottery, shell, and copper bells found in the area probably were acquired through trade.

Park Service archeologist Bruce Anderson has also added to these interpretations following a comprehensive survey of Wupatki. Anderson and his crews recorded some 2,600 sites in the monument itself, and the ceramics they found showed Anasazi, Sinagua, Cohonina, and Prescott cultures all represented. And despite the generally water-less environment, Anderson found evidence of extensive prehistoric farming.

The beauty of the ruins at Wupatki, set against the backdrop of the imposing San Francisco Peaks, is breath-taking. Many of the largest ones can be seen on a tour along the loop road that runs between Wupatki and Sunset Crater.

From the north entrance of Wupatki National Monument, *Lomaki* is the first ruin you encounter. A quarter-mile trail leads past the double Box Canyon Ruins at the mouth of an earthcrack. These rock fissures, associated with faults and volcanic activity, apparently were of special interest to the prehistoric dwellers. On the edge of another earthcrack nearby perches Lomaki, Hopi for

Lomaki

"Beautiful House." The Hopi names for most of the Wupatki sites were bestowed by archeologist Jesse Walter Fewkes, who excavated here at the turn of the century. Lomaki was built around A.D. 1192, about the time construction ended at Wupatki Pueblo. Dressed blocks of Kaibab limestone and sandstone boulders were used. Expansion of Lomaki is evidenced in the wall joinery and in the masonry styles. Crisp square corners show the fine rock work, and a large doorway provides entry into Lomaki's nine rooms.

Down the road from Lomaki, the ruins of the *Citadel* encircle a rubbly basalt butte, with *Nalakihu* at its base. The Citadel may have been built for defense. Nalakihu is more mysterious—ten rooms in it were burned, and buried in them were owl bones along with pottery storage jars made in the Prescott area.

A three-mile spur road off the main park road leads to *Wukoki*, "Big House." This three-story pueblo rises elegantly out of the Moenkopi Sandstone, the rock which prehistoric architects used to build Wukoki nearly 800 years ago. Fewkes speculated that one or two families lived here for many years.

Wupatki Pueblo

Wupatki Pueblo itself is the centerpiece of the monument. Construction began at this site around A.D. 1120 and ended by 1195. The largest ruin in the area, Wupatki eventually reached four stories high and contained about a hundred rooms. The pueblo was located to take advantage of one of the few perennial springs in the area.

A self-guided trail leads out from behind the visitor center, winding through the pueblo and out to a prehistoric amphitheater and a ballcourt, where people likely came from miles around to play ceremonial games similar to ones known in Mesoamerica. The presence of these structures indicates that Wupatki may have been a center of some kind during its height. However, around the end of the tenth century, Wupatki was completely abandoned.

LOCATION: North entrance 40 miles north of Flagstaff, off Highway 89. ACCESS: 36-mile paved loop road between Wupatki and Sunset Crater national monuments. Most ruins accessible by paved road; a few by short trail. FEE: None at Wupatki entrance.

CONTACT: Superintendent
             Wupatki National Monument
             2717 N. Steves Blvd. Suite 3
             Flagstaff, AZ 86004
             (602) 556-7134

PUERCO RUIN,
PETRIFIED FOREST NATIONAL PARK

Most people know of Petrified Forest National Park for its storied reserves of beautiful petrified wood. Others before us also appreciated the gemlike rock. Near Puerco

Petrified National Monument

Ruin in the central part of the park, glittering piles of chipped stone have been found at what was probably a prehistoric rock quarry. Almost all the chips in this "lithic scatter," as archeologists term it, are of petrified wood. This abundant, easily worked material was preferred for many of the tools of these stone-age people.

But there is more here than piles of chipped stone. On a sandstone bench above the Puerco River rise the ten-inch-thick walls of a large village of Puerco Ruin. Some of the seventy-five rooms of this trapezoid-shaped pueblo are partly reconstructed and open for public view. Rooms for living, storage and milling, and ceremonies have been identified at Puerco. At its height, perhaps eighteen families lived here.

People occupied Puerco at two different times—from A.D. 1100 to 1200, and again in the 1300s. It is one of the few sites in the region that was still inhabited in the fourteenth century. The final abandonment appears to have been slow and deliberate, and Puerco residents probably moved east to Zuni and north to the Hopi Mesas. The great mixture of pottery types found here indicates that people of several different southwestern cultures—Anasazi, Mogollon, and perhaps Sinagua—either lived or traded at Puerco.

In this high desert environment people sustained themselves by farming and hunting. They grew corn and cotton on the mesa tops and along the riverbed, most often where moisture-holding sand dunes accumulated. Water for their crops came mostly from rain, which amounted to only about eight inches a year. On their hunts, they pursued swift pronghorn that sped across the shortgrass prairie, and small rabbits that hid under the saltbushes.

Puerco Ruin

Petroglyphs on boulders at Puerco provide convincing evidence that residents kept track of time by watching the sun. At the summer solstice a beam of sunlight strikes a particular point on a spiral drawing on one rock. As people did six hundred years ago, visitors may still observe this phenomenon at Puerco on the days surrounding the solstice.

Puerco Ruin is the major archeological site open in

Petrified Forest National Park, but it is only one of many that have been recorded. Hundreds of sites are known, including an early Basketmaker pithouse site called Flattop at the south end of the park. A fine collection of prehistoric rock art can be seen at nearby Newspaper Rock.

LOCATION: 5 miles south of Interstate 40.
ACCESS: Parking area and ruin on east side of main road through Petrified Forest National Park. FEE: Entrance fee to park; none to ruin itself. Visitors to Puerco Ruin are reminded to stay on paved trails in the ruins area, not to remove any artifacts, and not to touch petroglyphs.

CONTACT: Superintendent
             Petrified Forest National Park,
             Arizona 86028
             (602) 524-6228

HOMOLOVI RUINS STATE PARK

The beauty of Homolovi is subtle. On the windswept edge of the Painted Desert, Homolovi asks time of a person, to absorb the vast sweep of seemingly featureless land. This important archeological area sits only a few miles north of the town of Winslow, Arizona, and knowing of its existence adds a human depth to what at first may appear an uninhabitable landscape. Protected within the 10,000 acres of Homolovi Ruins State Park are four separate prehistoric villages and two satellites—Cottonwood and Chevelon—strung along the Little Colorado River. Homolovi is a Hopi word which means "place of the mounds." Certain Hopi clans say that Homolovi was their last stopping place before they gained permission to settle on the Hopi mesas where they now live. Oral tradition holds that the ruins are the footprints of their ancestors, the *hisatsinom*, and they mark the boundaries of traditional Hopi territory.

The four major pueblos open for public visitation include Homolovi I, II, III, and IV. A short paved trail leads to

Corrugated pottery

Homolovi II, high on a sandstone mesa on the east side of the Little Colorado. From the mesa-top rooms, you can survey a 360-degree panorama, taking in the Painted Desert to the north, the Little Colorado River Valley and San Francisco Peaks to the west, and Anderson Mesa to the south.

The fourteenth-century pueblo of Homolovi II contained nearly 800 rooms (five of which are excavated and open to view) organized around the East, West, and Central plazas. Once two to three stories high, Homolovi II was occupied between A.D. 1250 and 1450. Artifacts found at the site—including obsidian, turquoise, shell, copper bells, and pottery from outside the area—suggest that Homolovi II functioned as a redistribution center for the region. Along a primitive trail near Homolovi II are a number of petroglyphs pecked into the boulders, including various clan symbols.

Homolovi I, just upstream from Homolovi II, consisted of a 250-room, three-story pueblo with rectangular plaza. People lived there from A.D. 1250 to 1400. A pithouse village which predates the pueblo by about six hundred years was also excavated near this location. The site has now been backfilled.

Homolovi III and IV are situated on the west side of the river. Homolovi III, a hamlet of thirty to forty rooms, is the smallest of the four major sites. It was occupied, abandoned, and then reoccupied seasonally. A great kiva, a larger version of the small rectangular ceremonial structures found at many sites, was built here. Homolovi IV is a pueblo of about 100 rooms that step up a butte just downstream from Homolovi III. Excavations in the 1980s indicate that it was probably the first pueblo of the four at Homolovi, dating to A.D.1100 to 1250.

Homolovi and surrounding sites have been known to

archeologists for a long time, at least since Jesse Walter Fewkes excavated in the area in the late 1890s for the Bureau of American Ethnology. He probed extensively in the burial grounds and sent back more than 2,500 artifacts to the National Museum. Since his time, illegal pothunting has taken a heavy toll on all the sites. Such vandalism was a primary motivation for protection of Homolovi in the state park system.

The park was officially dedicated in 1991, and a new visitor center is now complete. Plans are underway for more developments, including a system of trails to link the four major sites.

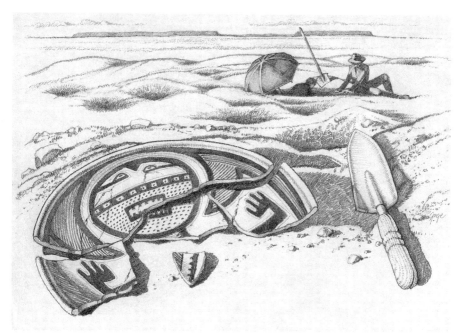

Pothunters of Homolovi, Arizona
Hopi mesas on horizon

LOCATION: 3 miles north of Winslow, Arizona, off Interstate 40. ACCESS: Travel north on Highway 87, the road to Second Mesa, and turn left (west) at the park signs. Homolovi Ruins State Park was still being developed at the time of this writing. FEE: Yes

CONTACT: Park Manager
             Homolovi Ruins State Park
             HC63-Box 5
             Winslow, AZ 86047
             (602) 289-4106

EL MORRO
NATIONAL MONUMENT

Inscription Rock

The record of people at "The Bluff"—the place the Spaniards called El Morro—is a rich one. Lured by the pool at its base, edged with cattails and fed by rain and snow, passersby could not resist leaving their autographs on the rock at El Morro in northwest New Mexico.

Though El Morro is best known for the historic writings, it also displays marks left by prehistoric dwellers. Rather than words, they left pictures on the rock. And on top of the rock were two large pueblos. The nearby Zuni Indians still call it Atsinna, "place of writing on the rock," their name both for El Morro and for the large ruin perched on top of the massive sandstone bluff. Zunis say the rock art and the pueblo were the works of their ancestors, who farmed here at 7,200 feet above sea level a thousand years ago.

The inscriptions at El Morro give voice to history. Spanish governors and priests stood before the great rockface and recorded their passing, most often prefacing their scratchings with the phrase *paso por aqui*, "he passed by here." Spanish governor and expeditioner Don Juan de Oñate was the first and most famous European to do so, in 1605. Joining his name are those of Don Francisco Manuel de Silva Nieto in 1629, Diego de Vargas in 1692, and General Juan Paez Hurtado in 1736. Representatives of the U.S. Army followed—most notably Lieutenants James Simpson in 1849 and Edward Beale, with his strange entourage of camels, ten years later. Settlers traveling westward, too, would probably never have been able to complete their journeys without the water shaded by El Morro.

All who left their inscriptions probably saw the Indian rock art etched into the face of El Morro—abstract zigzag lines and animal shapes that resembled strange sheep. They might also have remarked upon the depressions cut into the rock, serving as ladders just large enough for a foot or hand to gain hold and climb the rock. These were the shortcuts the mesa-top dwellers took to reach the waterhole from their pueblos.

Today a paved asphalt trail continues past the rock writings another mile and a half. It is a steep climb, and at this elevation is not advised for people with heart or respiratory problems. But there are plenty of stops along the way to gaze out on the magnificent Zuni Mountains and the El Morro Valley. The rewards are worth the short strain—a hummingbird may dive-bomb you, or a lizard might skitter by on the rock. The trail offers a geology lesson too, as it passes through the Jurassic-aged Zuni Formation into the Cretaceous Dakota Sandstone that caps the mesa.

Once on top of the mesa, the route meanders along the rolling bare rock, around the head of the ponderosa-filled box canyon, and finally to the main attraction, the ruins. There are two on either side of the canyon, the first unexcavated, the second partly excavated. The second one is Atsinna, a large pueblo that housed perhaps 1,500 people at its peak in the 1300s. Sixteen of Atsinna's 800 rooms have been excavated and stabilized, including both a circular and a square kiva. The pueblo may once have reached three stories on one side.

Archeologists Richard and Nathalie Woodbury excavated Atsinna in the late 1950s. They found that the Anasazi reused this site, taking stones from an earlier building and using them to construct Atsinna. The architectural style is reminiscent of Chaco Canyon, north of El Morro. A square plaza was surrounded first by single-story then by double-story rooms. The pueblo's solid outer wall suggests a defensive posture. Though few whole pots were found, the Woodburys did excavate many stone tools.

Only two generations of prehistoric people lived at Atsinna. The town was abandoned in the late 1300s, and the inhabitants likely moved westward about twenty-five miles to the Zuni pueblos. At the lower altitude there, crops may have fared better than at Atsinna. But the true cause of abandonment is still a matter of conjecture.

LOCATION: 58 miles southeast of Gallup and 43 miles west of Grants, New Mexico. ACCESS: Just south of New Mexico Highway 53. FEE: Yes

CONTACT: Superintendent
El Morro National Monument
Route 2, Box 43
Ramah, NM 87321-9603
(505) 783-4226

Agate House, Petrified Forest National Park, Pueblo III structure built of petrified wood

Polychrome pottery shards from Hawikuh

Rectangular Kiva, Atsinna Pueblo

Monument Valley Tribal Park

Entrance to the historic Hubble Trading Post

Old Zuni Mission, Zuni Pueblo (rebuilt 1968)

Contemporary Zuni pictographs circa 1930, Village of the Great Kivas

Polychrome bowl with ladle, Edge of the Cedars State Park

INDIAN RESERVATIONS

ZUNI RESERVATION

The same Spaniards who left their names on the rock at nearby El Morro also knew of the Indians living to the west. They had come to the region in search of the elusive Seven Cities of Cibola, which they had heard were built of gold. There were not actually seven, but six, pueblos at Zuni. And to the Spaniards' dismay, they were not made of gold but simply of stone and mud.

The Zunis, peaceful farmers and active traders, did not get along with the Spaniards. In 1539 Fray Marcos de Niza's scout Estevan was killed at the Zuni pueblo of Hawikku, and in the following year the Zuni were defeated there in a large battle with Coronado. (Coronado was seriously injured in the fighting.) On their shuttlings between Mexico and Santa Fe, the Spaniards spent a good deal of time trying to protect their vulnerable missionaries sent to colonize the resistant Zunis.

Friction between the Spaniards and the Zunis worsened, culminating in the Pueblo Revolt of 1680. The Zunis then left their pueblos and moved to nearby mesa tops, often seeking refuge on Dowa Yalanne, or Corn Mountain. Zunis say this was the mountain where they went to escape a great flood. After 1692, the people finally were forced together into one town called Halona, what is now Zuni Pueblo.

The *Ashiwi*, as the Zuni call themselves, now live on a 420,619-acre reservation in a beautiful part of northwest New Mexico, near the Arizona border. The sweet scent of piñon smoke is ever-present in the air at Zuni, floating from the *hornos*, beehive-shaped adobe ovens in which bread is baked; chiles and melons are sold at stands along the roads.

A famous landmark, the Old Mission Church in the center of the pueblo, is a reminder of the Catholic presence at Zuni. Originally built by Franciscans in 1629, the mission was destroyed in the 1680 revolt and rebuilt several times through the next three centuries. Through efforts of the Catholic Church, Zuni Tribe, and National Park Service, the adobe brick church was completely restored and reopened for use in 1970.

Old Mission Church

Zuni artist Alex Seowtewa, with his sons Kenneth and Edwin, have spent twenty years painting a series of murals high on the walls inside the church. If he is there, the elder Seowtewa will try to explain the meaning of his paintings to visitors. Advised by Zuni elders about the kachina murals that formerly decorated the walls, Mr. Seowtewa set out to paint similar ones. His scenes depict in colorful detail the kachinas that appear during the Shalako dances at Zuni in winter. Other parts of the mural depict the rites of spring, summer, and fall.

LOCATION: Zuni Pueblo and Old Mission Church are located on NM 53, 35 miles south of Gallup. ACCESS: The church is open to the public, and mass is celebrated every Sunday morning. FEE: No; donation accepted

Traditional Zuni religious dances are often open to the public, but can be entered only by permission. Contact the Pueblo of Zuni office to determine whether outsiders are allowed. A fee is charged for photographing in and around Zuni Pueblo. Photo permits may be obtained at the Pueblo of Zuni Tribal Building on Highway 53 Monday through Friday. The Zunis are accomplished potters and jewelers, and their arts and crafts can be found at several stores at the pueblo.

CONTACT: Pueblo of Zuni
P.O. Box 339
Zuni, NM 87327
(505) 892-4481

Zuni has been known among archeologists for a long time. Albert Kroeber and Leslie Spier visited Zuni in the late nineteenth and early twentieth centuries. Another archeologist, Frank Hamilton Cushing, lived with the Zuni for four years and was initiated into one of their most prestigious societies, the Priesthood of the Bow.

Cushing's stenographer, Frederick W. Hodge, launched a monumental archeological program at Zuni in 1917, specifically at the prehistoric pueblo of *Hawikku*. The ruins of this famous site, the first Zuni village visited by Europeans in what is now the United States, are located about fifteen miles south of Zuni Pueblo. Register at the Zuni Archeology Program office before heading to Hawikku. Much of what is visible of Hawikku's 340 rooms and mission was excavated by Hodge.

To reach Hawikku, turn south off Highway 53 at the Halona Store onto Zuni Route 2 (the road to Ojo Caliente). Continue south on this all-weather gravel road for about 12.5 miles. Turn right (west) onto Zuni Route 21 and go about one mile to a parking area at the site.

The other site open to public visitation is the *Village of the Great Kivas*, located northeast of Zuni Pueblo in Nutria Canyon. Excavated in 1930 by Frank H. H. Roberts of the Smithsonian Institution, this site has been identified as a

Petroglyphs, Village of the Great Kivas

Chacoan outlier, based on its time of occupation, architecture, and kiva styles. The walls are core and veneer masonry, and the two large great kivas are outside the pueblo itself. People lived at the village between A.D.1000 and 1030. On the rim of the mesa north of the room block is a petroglyph panel.

To reach Village of the Great Kivas, take Highway 53 north out of Zuni to NM 602. Turn right (north) onto 602 and continue for 3.2 miles. Turn right (east) onto Zuni Route 7, an improved dirt road that can be muddy and slick when wet. Travel about 3.1 miles up Zuni Route 7 (the road to Nutria Reservoir and Campground).

Just before the reservoir, turn left (west) on a dirt road that leads about 150 yards to a tree-covered knoll on the north edge of a side canyon. The site is on the knoll.

Before heading to Hawikku or Village of the Great Kivas, contact the office of the Zuni Archeology Program for a permit. They may be reached at (505) 782-4814.

Contemporary Pictographs at Village of the Great Kivas

HOPI MESAS

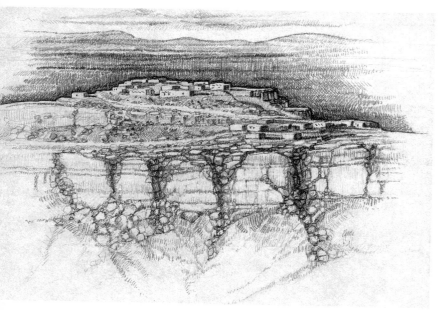

Shipolovi on Second Mesa

In the 1600s Spanish missionaries established themselves among the Hopi Indians in northeast Arizona. By 1680, resistance to the Spaniards had grown among all the pueblos, until finally they felt moved to declare their independence. Pope, a member of the Rio Grande pueblos, was to lead an uprising. Runners would carry a knotted cord to each pueblo; when the final knot was reached, a mass attack was to be launched. But the secret leaked, and an early surprise attack was staged that became known as the Pueblo Revolt of 1680. After the revolt, many Hopis sought security on the tops of their First, Second, and Third mesas.

The Spaniards had first contacted the Hopi at Awatovi, "Place of the Bow." Pedro de Tovar and his conquistadors arrived there in 1540. In 1629, Franciscan Father Porras built Mission San Bernardino on Antelope Mesa near Awatovi. This mission was destroyed and the Spanish priests killed in the 1680 revolt.

The Spanish Reconquest thirty years later brought priests once again. The chief at Awatovi, dissatisfied with those Hopis who converted to Christianity, wanted to send an unmistakable message to them and to the priests. Hopi men were assembled in the village kiva and shot with arrows. The kiva was burned with them inside. The final destruction of Awatovi, ironically, took place at the hands of other Hopis.

This famous landmark, now damaged by looters and by the elements, is the object of stabilization efforts by the Hopi Cultural Preservation Office and National Park Service. They hope to repair stone work and backfill trenches left open by the Peabody Museum's 1938 archeological excavations. Donations for the work are being accepted through the "Landmarks at Risk" program.

More information on the Awatovi project can be obtained through the Hopi Cultural Preservation Office, P.O. Box 123, Kykotsmovi, AZ 86039, (602) 734-2441. Awatovi and all other archeological sites on the Hopi Reservation are closed to nontribal members except by permit. Contact the cultural preservation office for requirements.

The Hopis say they arrived at First, Second and Third mesas through a series of migrations. Various clans arrived at different times from all points of the compass—from Mesa Verde and Chaco, Hovenweep, Betatakin, Keet Seel, and Homolovi. The Creator, *Maasaw*, instructed each clan when to continue it's journey, sometimes sending signs in the form of bright falling stars. The people always knew, by Maasaw's prophecy, that these mesas were their final destination.

The Snake Clan was the first to come, more than a thousand years ago. By A.D. 1275, at least thirty-five villages were already established on and around the mesas. Today some seven thousand Hopis live in a dozen autonomous villages on their one-and-a-half-million-acre reservation.

The Hopis are a welcoming but private people. Visitors should stop first at the Hopi Cultural Center on Second Mesa, which includes a museum that tells about the people, their history, and their arts and crafts. On the menu at the nearby restaurant are blue corn flakes for breakfast and traditional hominy stew for lunch.

Walpi -- from Dwellers at the Source, *book by William Webb and Robert Weinstein*

Visitors are also welcome in the individual villages, but should remain on the main streets and in the plazas. Do not venture off onto footpaths or disturb any shrines. Guides can be contacted at the community center at each village. Hopi pottery, baskets, jewelry, and kachina dolls often can be purchased from the individual makers in their homes.

- First Mesa Villages: Hano, Sichomovi, Walpi, Polacca
- Second Mesa Villages: Shungopavi, Shipaulovi, Mishongnovi
- Third Mesa Villages: Hotevilla, Bacavi, Kykotsmovi, Old Oraibi (believed to be the longest continuously occupied village in the United States), and Moenkopi (an outlying village near Tuba City)

The Hopis generously allow outsiders to view some of their ceremonial dances, which mark important times on their seasonal calendar. To see these dances is to see ritual that has been passed down through an oral tradition for a thousand years. The Cultural Center on Second Mesa is the best contact for times and places of the dances and to find out whether a particular ceremony is open to the public. Perhaps the best advice is to remain patient and inconspicuous; and remember always that these are religious observances. Dress and demeanor should honor that. Photographing, sketching, and recording are prohibited at all times at Hopi.

Hopi Orge Kachina

LOCATION: Along Highway 264, 65 miles north of Winslow, Arizona. ACCESS: Cultural Center is along main highway; villages accessible on paved, but often narrow, winding roads. FEES: Entrance fee to museum; guide fees vary from village to village.

CONTACT: Hopi Cultural Center
             P.O. Box 7
             Second Mesa, Arizona 86043
             (602) 734-6650

Four Mile polychrome bowl, Homolovi I

NAVAJO NATION

At one time the Navajos and Apaches were part of the same group, the Southern Athapaskans. They migrated south from the Bering Sea area, though their actual route is a matter of debate. They split into two bands somewhere along the way, and the Navajos remained in the northern part of the Southwest, a land of sand dunes and colorful rock eroded into fantastic shapes. They were, and still are, an adaptable people.

Exactly when the Navajos actually arrived in the Four Corners is a point of debate among scholars. Some say as early as A.D. 1000, others, as late as 1525. Most believe that a few hundred years passed between the time of the Anasazi's departure and the entry of the Navajos. In any event, the Spaniards found Navajos settled in northern New Mexico in 1582, as evidenced by accounts of Antonio de Espejo's expedition of that year.

The Spaniards called these farming and hunting people Apache de Nabajo, which means "large planted fields." At the time, Navajos were growing maize and other crops in the canyons. The Navajos call themselves *Dinè*, the People. After the Pueblo Revolt of 1680, some Pueblos sought refuge among the Navajo, and, for a time they were allies. During the early 1700s, some even lived together at sites called pueblitos, in places such as Simon Canyon in the Gobernador section of northern New Mexico. Though they adopted some Pueblo ceramics and architecture, the Navajos continued to emerge as a separate and distinct people.

In their land, called Dinetah, the Navajo built hogans, circular or hexagonal homes of logs and mud and sometimes stone. After the Spaniards introduced the horse to them, Navajos became great riders; today rodeos are still among the biggest events on the reservation. The Navajo took to raising livestock—sheep, goats, and now cattle—a pursuit well-suited to their dispersed lifestyle. Warfare with the Spanish, Utes, and Pueblos became a way of life, more so than some wished.

The arrival of Europeans in the region in the 1800s, especially the United States Army, nearly destroyed the Navajo. In 1864 Brigadier General James H. Carleton succeeded in forcing thousands of Navajos on a 300-mile journey on foot to Fort Sumner (Bosque Redondo) in eastern New Mexico. This event, known as the Long Walk, was one of the bleakest periods in Navajo history. For four years, the Navajos were detained at Fort Sumner. Many died or suffered sickness and starvation. Finally, in 1868, the horrible experiment was brought to a close. Treaty talks began, and the original 3.4-million-acre Navajo Reservation was established, straddling the New Mexico-Arizona border. The reservation has been expanded throughout this century to nearly 17 million acres.

During the treaty negotiations, Barboncito, one of the early spokesmen for the Navajo, said, "I hope to God you will not ask me to go to any other country except my own. . . We do not want to go to the right or left, but straight back to our own country." Finally a ten-mile-long column of people moved west under cavalry escort. The Navajo were going home.

Barboncito, chief of the Navajos
From Navajo Roundup, *book by Lawrence Kelly*

During the next century the Navajo saw great changes in their lives. One of the major ones was the arrival of Anglo traders and trading posts. A tribal government was formed in 1923. In the 1930s the United States government ordered huge numbers of Navajo sheep killed to eliminate overgrazing. The Native American Church, whose rituals include ingestion of peyote cactus, spread among Navajos, which some saw as a threat to traditional ceremonies.

The coming of missionaries, paved roads in the 1960s, television, and tourism have all brought change to the Navajo Reservation. Navajos have also been greatly

affected by development of coal, oil, natural gas, uranium and other minerals on the reservation.

In 1990, the official census reported 143,000 Navajos living on the reservation. Many others have left the reservation for cash jobs in border towns like Flagstaff, Farmington, and Gallup.

The 25,000-square-mile Navajo Reservation is filled with Anasazi ruins, including some of the most spectacular cliff dwellings in the Four Corners region. Visits to Navajo Nation archeological sites require a permit from the Navajo Nation Historic Preservation Department, P.O. Box 2898, Window Rock, AZ 86515 (602) 871-6437. At the time of this writing, no sites were open for general public visitation.

Hogan at Standing Cow Ruin, Canyon De Chelly

Some of the intriguing pueblitos of Dinetah, including the *Simon Canyon Recreation Area* east of Farmington, New Mexico, are open to the public. Most are accessible by dirt roads that vary in condition, depending on maintenance and weather. For more information, contact Bureau of Land Management, Farmington Resource Office, 1235 LaPlata Highway, Farmington, NM 87401, (505) 327-5344.

NAVAJO TRIBAL MUSEUM

The town of Window Rock, Arizona, became the capital of the Navajo Nation in the 1930s. None other than John Collier, the commissioner of Indian Affairs who ordered the hated livestock reduction program, was responsible for its designation. Now, tribal headquarters and nearby St. Michael's Mission and Fort Defiance

St. Michael's Mission

form a center of activity on the reservation.

The Navajo Tribal Museum in Window Rock, housed in the same building as the Arts and Crafts Cooperative, is a small but well done facility. Excellent exhibits on Navajo history, creation stories, weaving, silver, and pottery crafts, and a fully stocked bookstore make this a good introduction to the reservation.

LOCATION: On the north side of Highway 264, near junction with Highway 12, in Window Rock, AZ.
FEE: None

CONTACT: Navajo Tribal Museum
c/o Navajo Nation
Historic Preservation Department
P.O. Box 2898, Hwy 264
Window Rock, AZ 86515
(602) 871-6673

MONUMENT VALLEY TRIBAL PARK

Totem Pole, Monument Valley

The 30,000-acre Monument Valley Tribal Park was established as the first park on the Navajo Reservation in 1958. Monument Valley is famous for the cathedral-like buttes and spires, eroded from volcanic rock and sandstone: Agathla, "Place of the Scraping of Hides," which Kit Carson named El Capitan, rises up like a giant palm on the edge of Monument Valley. Geologically, El Capitan is different from most of the other formations. It is a volcanic neck, while most of the buttes and mesas are eroded from cliffs of DeChelly Sandstone.

Within the tribal park other named buttes rise—the matching North and South Mittens; Merrick Butte, named for a miner who was killed nearby by Paiutes in 1879, and whose bones were picked clean by buzzards and coyotes; Elephant and Camel buttes; the Three Sisters; and Spearhead and Rain God mesas. Dark green bands of juniper trees and sculpted sand dunes ring the bases of the thousand-foot sandstone monoliths.

Navajos still live in scattered settlements amid the buttes and mesas of Monument Valley. Traditional hogans, with sheep corral and summer ramada, make up a typical homeplace of an extended family. Grandmothers, dressed in rich velveteen shirts and tiered skirts, still herd sheep, weave rugs, and make frybread on outdoor woodstoves.

Monument Valley was memorialized in celluloid by Hollywood director John Ford, who shot *Stagecoach* and a number of other westerns there in the 1930s and 1940s. A point bearing his name can be seen along the road in Monument Valley.

LOCATION: Off Highway 163, on Arizona/Utah border, between Kayenta, Arizona, and Mexican Hat, Utah. ACCESS: Visitor Center and campground located five miles east of Highway 163; from visitor center, a 17-mile unpaved loop road leads through park. FEE: Yes

CONTACT: Navajo Nation Parks &
           Recreation Department
           P.O. Box 308
           Window Rock, AZ 86515
           (602) 871-6645

Many Monument Valley visitors also stop at *Goulding's Trading Post*. The historic post, located at the foot of Big Rock Door Mesa just west of the Monument Valley turnoff, has been transformed into a museum. Displayed inside are memorabilia of trading days, along with a film gallery with clips from John Ford's movies. The post was established in 1924 by Harry Goulding and his wife, Leone, known to most as "Mike." Open daily, April through October, with admission charge.

Three Sisters, Monument Valley

HUBBELL TRADING POST
NATIONAL HISTORIC SITE

After the Navajos returned to their homeland in 1868 from the Long Walk to Bosque Redondo, the trading post era dawned. Navajos came to the posts to trade their wool, sheep, rugs, and jewelry for flour and coffee, tobacco, calico, and canned pears. So strange was this fruit that the Navajo who came to Hubbell called them "apples-with-tails-on-them-in-a-can." Barter or a token system, rather than hard cash, furnished the means of exchange at most trading posts.

Gathered around the warm stove in the "bull pen" in the center of the room, Indians and traders would conduct business, gossip, and sometimes even receive or administer medical care. In this way, the outside world entered the Navajo consciousness. Traders also heavily influenced Navajo crafts—a rug weaver might be encouraged to use a red dye and different design, for example.

Among the most famous and admired traders was John Lorenzo Hubbell. Hubbell Trading Post, along Pueblo Colorado Wash, was purchased by John Lorenzo in 1878. Ganado, the town where it is located, was named for Ganado Mucho, a Navajo leader and friend of Hubbell's.

Now a national historic site operated by the National Park Service, Hubbell—the oldest continuously active trading post on the Navajo Reservation—provides insight into this significant part of Navajo history. Included within the 160-acre site is a visitor center, the trading post where Navajo rugs are stacked high (and are available for purchase), the Hubbell home, barn, chicken coop, and assorted farming equipment.

Park rangers lead tours through the cool, dark, heavy-timbered Hubbell home. The wooden floors are covered with huge Navajo rugs, the living room ceiling is lined with Indian baskets, and the walls exhibit scores of paintings by famous artists who visited this out-of-the-way spot. Many noted guests, including President Theodore Roosevelt, were hosted in the Hubbell dining room.

Inside the Hubbell visitor center, Navajo weavers show their patient skills at working with the colorful wools. The grounds of Hubbell may be seen on a self-guided tour, with a brochure available at the bookstore in the visitor center.

LOCATION: On Highway 264, in Ganado, Arizona. 55 miles northwest of Gallup, New Mexico. FEE: No

CONTACT: Superintendent
            Hubbell Trading Post National Historic Site
            P.O. Box 150
            Ganado, AZ 86505
            (602) 755-3475

Hubbell Trading Post is one of the few authentic trading posts left on the Navajo Reservation. Others, such as Inscription House in northeast Arizona and Oljeto in

southeast Utah, retain their character; but the posts are changing fast. The exteriors of some have been preserved, but on the counters inside are mostly modern goods such as soft drinks, disposable diapers, and videos.

Wagon at Hubbell Trading Post

UTE RESERVATIONS

The Ute Indians once claimed a huge part of Colorado, Utah, and northern New Mexico as their home. Before Europeans and Americans arrived in their homelands, Ute families were organized into bands. These small groups migrated into the mountains in spring and summer and back down to the valleys in the fall, in search of plants and game. Once they acquired horses from the Spaniards, the Utes knew a new kind of mobility. They could travel east to the Great Plains to hunt buffalo, from whose hides they made exquisite buckskin clothing.

By the 1850s, however, the Utes began to see settlers and miners entering their territory. In treaties with the U.S. government in 1863 and 1868, they ceded some lands but tried to hold on to others and to minimize the impact of the newcomers. But they were unsuccessful, and upon the signing of the Brunot Agreement in 1873, the Utes were removed from New Mexico to Colorado and Utah.

In Colorado, they now live on two small reservations. The 800,000-acre Southern Ute Reservation is home to the Mouache and Capote bands. The Weminuche band was left with 582,828 acres in the far southwest corner of the state, now known as the Ute Mountain Ute Reservation or Homeland.

SOUTHERN UTES

Southern Ute Beadwork

In 1877 the agency at Ignacio, Colorado, was established, now headquarters for the Southern Ute tribe. Inside a modern motel in Ignacio is a small museum, part of the *Southern Ute Indian Cultural Center*. The museum exhibits beautiful bead and leather work, crafts at which Ute Indians excelled. You can also see photographs of former Ute leaders in full dress regalia. Upon request, you may view the film, "The Ute Legacy," based on a scholarly history of the tribe. At the museum you may also obtain information on times of traditional tribal dances, such as the spring Bear Dance, that are open to the public.

LOCATION: Ignacio, Colorado, at Sky Ute Lodge on Highway 172, 24 miles southeast of Durango. Museum open year-round, seven days a week. FEE: No; donations accepted.

CONTACT: Southern Ute Indian Cultural Center
P.O. Box 737
Ignacio, CO 81137
(303) 563-4531

UTE MOUNTAIN UTES

Guide at Ute Mountain Tribal Park displays arrowheads

The Ute Mountain Utes administer the *Ute Mountain Tribal Park* and run day tours to Anasazi sites in the park. Though "discovered" in the late nineteenth century by the now-famous Wetherill brothers of Mancos, Colorado, some of the better-known tribal park sites, such as Eagle Nest House and Morris No. 5, were named and excavated in 1913 by archeologist Earl Morris of Aztec Ruins fame.

Around A.D. 1130 the Anasazi of this area began to choose the cliffs over the mesa tops for their living quarters. They left for a brief time, then returned in 1195 and started building again, until about 1240. The tribal park, though more remote and wild, is truly an extension of Mesa Verde. Its prehistory is one and the same with its more famous northern neighbor.

In addition to prehistoric sites, the tribal park also contains examples of rare, historic Ute rock art. A good deal of this was done by a chief named Jack House who signed his name to some of his work.

Primarily a primitive area, the tribal park is open only for tours (operated by Ute guides and requiring advance reservations), day hikes, or backpacking. Hikers must obtain a permit from the tribe.

LOCATION: Tribal headquarters, Towoac, Colorado, Highway 666, 15 miles south of Cortez. ACCESS: Main ruins on tour are 40 miles off paved roads, on good gravel. Individuals drive own vehicles. FEE: Yes

CONTACT:　Ute Mountain Ute Tribal Park
　　　　　Towoac, CO　81334
　　　　　Toll-free 1-800-565-9653

MUSEUMS

Edge of the Cedars State Park museum

EDGE OF THE CEDARS
STATE PARK AND RUINS

Even before you enter the doors of the museum at Edge of the Cedars you know this is a lively place. In the courtyard reside sculptures by southeast Utah artist Joe Pachak. The nearly life sized concrete and wire figures are two-dimensional rock art images transformed into three dimensions. Pachak calls the exhibit "Catch Something Running," an appropriate name for these animated flute players, bighorn sheep, and Antman climbing down a ladder into a kiva.

Sculpture Garden

Once inside Edge of the Cedars museum, you can view frequently changing photographic exhibits. The bold, colorful permanent exhibits cover the Anasazi, Ute, Navajo, and Anglo cultures of San Juan County, Utah. An excellent educational display details how prehistoric pottery was made and painted, with an incredible pottery collection on exhibit.

Once through the museum, visitors may continue outside along a wooden boardwalk through a partially excavated Anasazi village overlooking Westwater Canyon. The site consists of six complexes, but only Complex 4, a large block of rooms with a great kiva, and part of Complex 6 have been revealed by excavation. People lived here from A.D. 750 to 1220, their tan sandstone rooms taking in the full view of the imposing Abajo Mountains. The great kiva associated with Complex 4 is significant because such structures are rarely found this far north, a hint that this site may be a Chacoan outlier.

Edge of the Cedars museum

LOCATION: 660 West 400 North, Blanding, Utah, on northwest edge of town. ACCESS: Turn west off Highway 191, follow yellow arrows painted on roads. FEE: Yes

CONTACT: Edge of the Cedars State Park
            P.O. Box 788
            Blanding, UT 84511-0788
            (801) 678-2238

Edge of the Cedars museum

CROW CANYON ARCHAEOLOGICAL CENTER

Archeologist at Castle Rock

A few miles north of Cortez, Colorado, sits the tastefully designed campus of the Crow Canyon Archaeological Center, complete with dining room and log hogans that serve as student housing. Founded in 1984 as a nonprofit organization for archeological research and education, Crow Canyon conducts day and weeklong programs for the public. Adults and children, students and teachers, can gain excavation and laboratory experience, enroll in workshops, and travel to archeological sites in the Southwest.

The center's "Cultural Explorations" are workshops with Native American instructors who teach weaving, pottery, basketry, and sometimes even gourmet cooking—Anasazi style. On other explorations, participants visit sites such as Chaco Canyon and Zuni Pueblo, or tour the Four Corners region during the autumn color season. "Southwest Seminars" are seven-day travel sessions with professional archeologists, covering topics such as prehistoric rock art and historic Hispanic art in the Four Corners.

LOCATION: 5 miles north of Cortez, CO. ACCESS: West of Highway 666, follow signs to the Center. FEE: Varies with program. Covers tuition, food, lodging, and transportation after arrival in Cortez. For a current catalog contact:

CONTACT: Crow Canyon Archaeological Center
23390 County Road K
Cortez, CO 81321
(303) 565-8975 or 1-800-422-8975

One of Crow Canyon's major projects was excavation of nearby *Sand Canyon Pueblo*. This large village contains more than 300 rooms, ninety kivas, fourteen towers, and a rare triwall structure. The pueblo is almost entirely enclosed by a wall. It was occupied in the mid- to late 1200s, just before the Anasazi vacated the Mesa Verde region. Because of Sand Canyon's late occupation, research is focusing on the mystery of Anasazi abandonment of the Four Corners. A half-mile self-guiding trail leads through the ruin.

LOCATION: Approximately fifteen miles northwest of Cortez. ACCESS: On a series of county roads west of Highway 666; inquire at Anasazi Heritage Center or Crow Canyon Archaeological Center for directions. FEE: None.

The excavation of Sand Canyon is being conducted in cooperation with the Bureau of Land Management, which oversees the surrounding, larger Sand Canyon Archeological Area. For more information about additional sites, contact BLM, Federal Building, 701 Camino Del Rio, Durango, CO 81301, (303) 247-4082.

Participatory archeology is becoming a popular pastime in the Four Corners. Other sources for lectures, workshops, trips, and opportunities for hands-on excavations led by professionals are listed below. Contact each individually for current program and trip information:

White Mesa Institute
College of Eastern Utah/San Juan Campus
Blanding, UT 84511
(801) 678-2201

Four Corners School of Outdoor Education
P.O. Box 1029
Monticello, UT 84535
1-800-525-4456 OR (801) 587-2859

Canyonlands Field Institute
P.O. Box 68, 1320 S. Highway 191
Moab, UT 84532
(802) 259-7750

The Archaeological Conservancy
5301 Central Ave. NE Suite 1218
Albuquerque, NM 87108
(505) 982-3278

Museum of Northern Arizona
Route 4, Box 720
Flagstaff, AZ 86001
(602) 774-5211

Jim Judge
Archaeology Research Program
Fort Lewis College
Durango, CO 81301
(303) 247-7409

As part of Fort Lewis College's archeology program and field school, the public may observe students excavating the Pigg site. This seventy-room pueblo, part of the Lowry Complex, includes ten kivas, a plaza, tower, and intersecting roads. In the future the program may include training and public participation in the excavations. The site is located thirty miles northwest of Cortez, Colorado, adjacent to Lowry Pueblo.

Excavation at Pigg site

ANASAZI HERITAGE CENTER
DOMINGUEZ AND ESCALANTE RUINS

Anasazi Heritage Center

If you are interested in Four Corners archeology, specifically the Northern San Juan Anasazi, one of the best places to start is at the Anasazi Heritage Center just outside Dolores, Colorado. You will know even before entering the doors that this is no ordinary museum. The architecture of the building, constructed of fine sandstone masonry, is modeled after the D-shaped Pueblo Bonito at Chaco Canyon.

The 40,500-square-foot center houses exhibits, a theater, library, gallery, multi-use room, and bookshop. Out of view but much a part of the Center is a laboratory where some two million artifacts and documents are curated. The artifacts came from one of the largest salvage archeology projects in the Southwest, the Dolores Archaeological Program conducted before McPhee Dam was built on the Dolores River. Operated by the U.S. Bureau of Land Management, the Anasazi Heritage Center was built in 1989 as part of the Dolores project.

Many of the Dolores artifacts are exhibited in the museum, along with a full-sized, reconstructed Anasazi pithouse, graphic timeline of the development of Anasazi life and technology, and the hands-on Discovery Area where visitors may grind corn, view seeds of beeweed and cattail under microscopes, or learn how archeologists excavate a site.

Two important Anasazi sites—the *Dominguez* and *Escalante* ruins—can be seen outside the Anasazi Heritage Center along a one-mile roundtrip paved path. The ruins were first recorded by Fathers Francisco Atansio Dominguez and Silvestre Velez de Escalante on their journey from Santa Fe to California in 1776. They camped by the Dolores River in August of that year. On the thirteenth of the month Father Escalante noted in his journal "a small settlement" of ancient times on the south side of the river.

Escalante Ruin

The small settlement probably referred to what is now *Escalante Ruin* at the top of the hill. The ruin's architecture and masonry—with its block of rooms enclosing two kivas—are similar to those found in Chaco Canyon, nearly 200 miles south in New Mexico. The Escalante village is believed to be an outlier in the Chaco system. Chacoan people may have come here and built this as a trading center in A.D. 1129, but they stayed for only about a decade. Two groups of Mesa Verde people then reoccupied the site around A.D. 1150 and 1200.

Dominguez Ruin was discovered later, and excavated in 1975 and 1976. At the base of the hill in front of the Heritage Center, this four-room site with a kiva dates to A.D. 1123. It shows Northern San Juan Anasazi rather than Chacoan architecture. A fascinating burial of a thirty-five-year-old woman was found in the corner of one of the rooms. With her were a number of offerings, including nearly 7,000 beads, a frog pendant, and pottery that hint she was a person of high social rank.

LOCATION: Ten miles north of Cortez, CO, Three miles west of Dolores, CO. ACCESS: On north side of Highway 184. FEE: None.

CONTACT: Anasazi Heritage Center
27501 Highway 184
Dolores, CO 81323
(303) 882-4811

MUSEUM OF NORTHERN ARIZONA

   Harold Colton, the man who first defined the Sinaqua
culture, also founded the Museum of Northern Arizona in
1928. Situated in a forest of ponderosa pines on the edge of
Flagstaff, Arizona, MNA, as it's known, bills itself as the
gateway to the great physiographic region known as the
Colorado Plateau, of which the Four Corners is a major
portion.

   MNA contains a permanent anthropological exhibit,
"Native Peoples of the Colorado Plateau," which takes
visitors through 12,000 years of human history, from the
earliest hunter-gatherers, to the Anasazi, to the modern-
day Hopi, Navajo, Havasupai, and Hualapai. A fine-art
gallery has been added, displaying some of the museum's
holdings of easel art and sculpture. The outdoor courtyard
features plants of seven different life zones from the Grand

Canyon to the top of the nearby San Francisco Peaks. Newly revamped geology and biology exhibits opened in 1992.

MNA hosts three popular annual events-the Zuni, Hopi, and Navajo shows, which feature award winning arts and crafts. It also sponsors an active educational program, with a good deal of focus on Four Corners archeology.

LOCATION: U.S. Highway 180, north of Flagstaff, Arizona. FEE: Yes

CONTACT: Museum of Northern Arizona
            Route 4, Box 720
            Flagstaff, AZ 86001
            (602) 774-5211

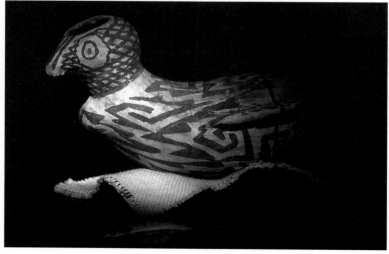

Bird effigy, Museum of Northern Arizona

Pottery held together with original yucca strapping, Edge of the Cedars

SUGGESTED READINGS

Amsden, Charles Avery. *Prehistoric Southwesterners From Basketmaker to Pueblo.* Los Angeles, CA: Southwest Museum, 1949.

Berry, Michael S. *Time, Space and Transition in Anasazi Prehistory.* Salt Lake City, UT: University of Utah Press, 1982.

Brody, J.J. *The Anasazi: Ancient Indian People of the American Southwest.* New York: Rizzoli, 1990.

Cordell, Linda S. *Prehistory of the Southwest.* Orlando, FL: Academic Press 1984

Ferguson, William M., and Arthur H. Rohn. *Anasazi Ruins of the Southwest in Color.* Albuquerque, NM: University of New Mexico Press, 1987.

Gumerman, George J. *A View From Black Mesa: The Changing Face of Archaeology.* Tucson, AZ: University of Arizona Press, 1984.

Kidder, Alfred Vincent. *An Introduction to the Study of Southwestern Archaeology.* New Haven, CT: Yale University Press rev. ed. 1962. Originally published 1924.

Lister, Robert H., and Florence C. Lister. *Chaco Canyon: Archaeology and Archaeologists.* Albuquerque, NM: University of New Mexico press, 1981.
_____. *Those Who Came Before.* Tucson, AZ: Southwest Parks and Monuments Association, 1983.

Matlock, Gary. *Enemy Ancestors: The Anasazi World with a Guide to Sites.* Flagstaff, AZ: Northland Press, 1988.

Noble, David Grant, ed. "Understanding the Anasazi of Mesa Verde and Hovenweep." *Exploration, Annual Bulletin of the School of American Research,* Santa Fe, NM, 1985.

_____."New Light on Chaco Canyon." *Exploration, Annual Bulletin of the School of American Research,* Santa Fe, NM, 1984.

_____. "Tse Yaa Kin: Houses Beneath the Rock." *Exploration: Annual Bulletin of the School of American Research,* Santa Fe, NM, 1986.

Ortiz, Simon, ed. *Handbook of North American Indians,* Southwest, vol. 9. Washington, DC: Smithsonian Institution, 1979.

Pike, Donald G., text; photographs by David Muench. *Anasazi: Ancient People of the Rock.* New York: Crown Publishers, 1974.

Widdison, Jerold G., ed. *The Anasazi: Why Did They Leave? Where Did They Go?* Proceedings of a panel discussion, Anasazi Heritage Center, Dolores, CO, June 1990. Albuquerque, NM: Southwest Natural and Cultural Heritage Association, 1991.

ACKNOWLEDGEMENTS

Many people deserve sincere thanks for their efforts in seeing this book to reality. Laurie Gruel of the San Juan National Forest Association maintained her faith throughout the process, which at times required great perseverance. San Juan National Forest acheologist Gary Matlock was there too, contributing his ideas, enthusiasm, and thorough review of the draft manuscript. Jim Fuge kept me going in many ways during the field work, and Tom and Sandra McMurray of Pika Graphics did a fine job of design and production. Thanks to Russell Martin, who put me onto this in the first place, and to my husband, Michael Collier, who spent three wonderful days in Grand Gulch with me. And finally, to the many individuals with agencies and tribes, too numerous to mention here, who readily provided information, permissions, and reviews. It is heartening to know of their stewardship of our cultural heritage.

--R.H.

Rose Houk is a freelance author and editor specializing in archeology, natural history, history, and travel. Publications include a series on Southwestern prehistory, *A Guide to the Natural History of Great Smoky Mountains*, *Dawn of the Dinosaurs*, *Painted Desert: Land of Light and Shadow*, and *Wildflowers of the American West*. She is a frequent contributor to *Arizona Highways* magazine. Rose has worked as an editor for the University of Arizona

Photo Michael Collier

Press and National Wildlife Federation, as a newspaper reporter, and as a ranger naturalist at Grand Canyon National Park. She lives in Flagstaff, Arizona.

Jim Fuge lives near Durango, Colorado. His paintings and photographs are of subjects throughout the southwest. "Doing the photography and illustrations for this guidebook was a great opportunity to visit these sites and think about the people who lived in them. I was continually impressed by their ability to thrive in this harsh land and by the esthetic qualities of the buildings and artifacts. Over the years new people have moved into the area. Only time

Photo Marie Leslie Fuge

will tell if; like the Anasazi, their descendants are still here 1,000 years from now."